THE IMAGE OF THE

Hermione Roff

THE IMAGE OF THE UNSEEN GOD

For Claire, Tom, Jenny, Ellen and Toby

First published 2009, Lancaster UK.
© Hermione Roff

Further copies available from hermione@roff.org.uk
Use in public worship welcomed, but please acknowledge source.

By the same author:

Reflective Interpersonal Therapy for Children and Parents
Wiley 2008   ISBN 978-0-470-98648-6

Typeset and cover design by John Roff

Cover picture:
'Draw Yourself' by Jamie

THE IMAGE OF THE UNSEEN GOD

The three sections of the book are inter-related.

The first section endeavours to think about biblical themes and seasons of the church's calendar as the revelation of the unseen God.

The second section thinks about the world and returns that thought through the lens of perceiving God in creation.

The third section takes the lives of ordinary children in our society, in all their sometimes shocking detail, and tries to discern the image of God within them and their circumstances.

This in turn reflects on the writer and the reader as being children of God alongside them.

Almighty God,
you have created the heavens and the earth
and made us in your own image:
teach us to discern your hand in all your works
and your likeness in all your children;
through Jesus Christ your Son our Lord,
who with you and the Holy Spirit reigns supreme over all things,
now and for ever.

Collect for the Second Sunday before Lent

THE IMAGE OF THE UNSEEN GOD

Section 1:

HE IS THE IMAGE OF THE UNSEEN GOD
Form us in the likeness of Your image……

Section 2:

JOURNEYING AS A CHILD OF GOD
Teach us to discern your hand in all your works……

Section 3:

¶SNAPSHOTS
and your likeness in all your children......

THE IMAGE OF THE UNSEEN GOD

HE IS THE IMAGE OF THE UNSEEN GOD

Form us in the likeness of Your image......

¶ CHRISTMAS

HE IS THE IMAGE OF THE UNSEEN GOD
Form us in the likeness of Your image . . . . .

Christmas Quartet

1. A Simple Gift

A simple gift,
Simply given,
So the simple, may
Simply live.

2. Stable

Heaven, stabilised on earth.
Stability centred at the core.
My life in You –
More stable.

3. Homelessness

If you live alone, whose
Feet will you wash?
Come Lord Jesus,
Dwell with me.
In my deep sense of
Homelessness, where I am
Shabbiest, find your
Manger, bring your
Love.

4. Mary

Let me be like you.
Let me receive the seed.
Let the Word take flesh
In me.

HE IS THE IMAGE OF THE UNSEEN GOD
Form us in the likeness of Your image......

5

Set-a-side at Christmas

Set-a-side in your heart a
Field, a
Field wild with clover,
Scented, hazy,
Tumbled about with
Butterflies, dipped and hollowed,
Spangled with daisies and
Long-stemmed buttercups,
Meadowsweet and
Wind-blown silken poppies. A
Field not neatly hedged or
Fixed by fence, but
One where you can
Fill your hat with
Sunshine and take it
Home.

Do not seek to
Profit by this field and it will
Surprise you with its
Colour and bloom, the way it
Blossoms into a
Free and airy space where the
Stranger can enter and become a
Friend instead of
Enemy.

Such a field was the one where
Shepherds sat, which
Glowed with angels' songs: where a
Stable grew out of the
Darkness: where
God set aside His
Power and came
Awesome as a Baby.

HE IS THE IMAGE OF THE UNSEEN GOD
Form us in the likeness of Your image......

6

Nativity

I will sing a song to the one I love, a
Song about His birth.

I heard God in the silence,
I listened to His voice.
In our encounter
His shadow fell across me.
I responded, and from my obedience,
Life burst forth.

Your wrinkled squashed-in face,
Your tiny fists and perfect toes.
I trace my finger over the
Curve of your cheek,
Smooth down the black shock of hair.
You gaze at me with
Eyes that mirror the intensity of
Unseen worlds: worlds still
Seen, still felt.
You snuffle into my breast with
Eager, hungry lips, and
Dream, contented, a trickle of
Warm milk escaping in a sigh the
Corner of your mouth.

Flesh and blood, flesh and blood,
My body broken, split open, for you.
My blood shed for you.
Water and blood issuing forth in a
Life-giving stream.

Terror rises in my heart as I
Gaze on your naked vulnerability.
My womb contracts with pain,
Strong pains that tighten and
Tauten the core of my being, turning
Blood into water, water into blood.

I can only hold you.
From some distant echoing depth I
Know how to hold you.
I hold your head,
Cradle your body,
Bind you in swaddling clothes,
Giving you memories of
Safety and security.

I will not allow any primitive agony of
Abandonment, of yearning, to
Weaken you.
I lift you, I gather you together, I
Protect you from dying, from
Losing all hope in
Relationship.

My son, my son,
How like your father you are –
How you will grow into His likeness.

For you, you too, will
Hear God and listen to His voice.
In your encounter the
Shadow of the cross will fall over you.
You will respond, and in your
Obedient response
Life will burst forth.

HE IS THE IMAGE OF THE UNSEEN GOD
Form us in the likeness of Your image.......

7

Away in a Manger

*(A neglected and deprived child reflects
on the meaning of this carol for him)*

Voice 1:
**Away in a manger,
no crib for a bed.**

Child:
I've got a mattress for my bed,
On the floor. I
Share it with my Dad.
I wish I could get away, away in a manger,
Get my own space.

Voice 1:
**The little Lord Jesus laid
down his sweet head.**

Child:
My head's not sweet. It's
Fierce, bruised, angry. It's a
Butt-head. (I butt walls, doors,
Mum, Dad,) a
Butt-head, not a smack head like my
Mum, like my Dad.

Voice 1:
**The stars in the bright sky
looked down where He lay.**

Child:
I look up at the stars you know.
I search the sky at night.
Standing by the window, waiting,
Listening, watching.
But my sky is black, not bright.
The stars are
Pale, (if I can see them at all)
Pale in the orange street light.
Still, sometimes, just sometimes,
I get the feeling that
Someone must be looking out for me.
They have to. Please.

Voice 1:
**The little Lord Jesus asleep
on the hay.**

Child:
My hay is needles,
Dirty, used.
A bit like hay really
Sharp and scratchy,
Dropped in the methy scripts
when they've had their
Fix, (that way they can score twice.)
I don't sleep much.

Voice 1:
**The cattle are lowing,
the baby awakes,
But little Lord Jesus
no crying He makes.**

Child:
Dad doesn't low, he bellows,
Drunk down the street he
Sways in front of me
Bleary, smeary eyes, but still with
Fists of iron – for my Mum.
I'm already awake, and no crying I make.
I'm frozen, churned sick.
I'm silent at the top of the stairs.
Watching.

Voice 1:
**The stars in the bright sky
looked down where He lay,
The little Lord Jesus
asleep on the hay.**

Child:
Keep looking down on me.
Even though I'm not asleep.
Even though I'm a butt-head.

Voice 1:
Be near me Lord Jesus,
I ask Thee to stay
Close by me for ever,
and love me I pray.

Child:
They say they love me.
I believe them when they say it.
When they curl up next to me,
crying,
Saying sorry.
They say they love me to bits, -
and I know that's
Right. I'm turning into
Bits in their love.
It's scary to say, but I don't know if
I can stand
Being in bits.
(If you're in bits you can't
stand, can you?
No-one could, could they?)
What would they do if I said,
'If this is love I'd rather try
something else'?
No. It's probably me.
Who could love me – a butt-head?
They try. They just got
someone who doesn't fit,
Who isn't lovable.

Voice 1:
Bless all the dear children
in Thy tender care

Child:
What is tender care?
Will someone tell me?
Perhaps I've got it and don't know.
How can you know unless
someone tells you?

Voice 1:
And fit us for heaven,
to live with Thee there.

Child:
I'll get fit.
I'd like to live.
Would there be room for a
butt-head?
(Not a smack head.)
Where is heaven?
I keep looking for it here on earth,
But it's hard on your own,
Hard on your own, when
you're seven.
Amen.

(smack head = drug addict:
methy script = methadone prescription:
score = inject.)

O Lord of Lords….

Ruler of the House of Israel, You
Come to us, housed in a stable.

Adonai of the cloud and burning bush, You
Burnish our souls with the
Blue, searing light of
Clarity.

Law-giver from the heights of Sinai, You
Lean out of a baby's eyes and
Grab us, with
Arms of outstretched
Love.

Even so, come Lord Jesus.

Joseph Speaks

It was not the news of a
Baby that hurt, (I
Loved her, and was inclined to
Believe her.) It was that
She
Did not think of
Me. How could she make such a
Momentous decision without
Consulting me? I thought she
Loved me, (I would
Die for her,) and yet she
Forgot me. I thought we were
Together, mind and
Soul and body, that our
Lives were bound as one,
She in me, I in her, - yet, her
Assumption was that I was
Nothing to do with it,
I did not enter the
Equation, - (she even asked
Who the father would be!)
How can I
Love this child who already
Divides and separates us?

I love her and so I have
Stayed. And this is how I
Find myself in a
Stable, enduring the
Silence, waiting in the
Darkness, for the
Eyes of my beloved to
Open and gaze on me.

I hear a
Rushing sound like water and a
Cry like life,
Life, bloody, raw and wet,
Steaming in the cold,
Slippery and glistening in the
Light of an angel's eyes.

From the mists and
Marshes of my mind
Blooms a flower of
Hope and love. I hear
My voice cry out,

'You are God's Son and
Mary's Son, and I will
Be like a father to You. I will
Teach You all I know of
Love and Grief, of
Patience and Fortitude, the
Mysterious strength of a
Person fashioned by
Wood and hammer and
Nails.

HE IS THE IMAGE OF THE UNSEEN GOD
Form us in the likeness of Your image ......

11

In the beginning

The stimulus was the
Silence of the
Locked garden. The
Cold ash of the
Burning bush, no longer even
Smouldering.
Darkness covering the
Land, stripping the world of
Colour and depth. In

Matters of love there is
Everything to be
Gained, everything to be
Lost. The
Word, uncreated and
Eternal in the mind of God
Waits. Then, the

Maid, in her
Innocence, said, 'Yes,' negating
Centuries of
Loss.
God opened His voice. The
Word raced and thrilled down
Human veins,
Fizzed and gathered in
Knots of sinew at
Wrist and ankle.
Pulsed through
Bone and marrow,
Synapses linking and
Catching, cells
Fusing, multiplying, dividing in a
Frenzy of creation. The
Memory of God, of
All He is,
Written in
Blood and bone,
Scattering in exultation and

Emerging in the
Cry from the manger, (the
Cry from the cross),
'Abba,
Father.' The

Burning bush
Flared into life, and in the
Language and
Meaning of
Love, the dawn of God's glory,
Set fire to the stars, and
Lit up the world.

HE IS THE IMAGE OF THE UNSEEN GOD
Form us in the likeness of Your image......

12

¶ EPIPHANY.

HE IS THE IMAGE OF THE UNSEEN GOD
Form us in the likeness of Your image......

13

The Four Kings

Gold splashes its light boldly
To and fro, flickering and reflecting
Its age-old wisdom as
One King recognises another.
He draws close
The more to shine within your
Encircling orb.
He thrills at the splendour no
Gold on earth can surpass.
Thrills, as The Word from ages past
Creates in him anew
(Another light, another time).

Frankincense,- the
Word, lingers like the curling
Smoke of candles guttering in the
Wind. His prayers like sighs
Shudder and faint at the
Intimate knowledge of such
Kingship, such power, such glory
Set before him
Face to face.
(Another face, another time).

But it is the third king I think of.
Did he break the precious casket of
Myrrh, over your tiny feet
So that the house was full of the
Fragrance?
In his wisdom, did He
Anoint you
Tenderly, and

Weeping, cover your infant body with his
Tears,
Wipe your soft limbs with his
Hair?
Every time Mary drew in that scent
It pierced her with the
Keenness of its fragrant
Homage.
(Another Mary, another time).

And I too, yearn, my Lord, my King, my
God, to
Savour you, taste you, as did those
Kings
(Another year, another time).

To reflect the gold of your presence
In this dark world.
Pray, the love prayer of
Frankincense,
Share the grievous joy of myrrh
Deep in the knowledge of your
Wisdom.
This year, this time.

HE IS THE IMAGE OF THE UNSEEN GOD
Form us in the likeness of Your image.....

15

The Gift

I presuppose that You will
Like my gift.
I take for granted that I can
Bring You my gift.
I assume that You are there to
Receive my gift.
I do not have the
Despair of knowing that there is a
Void at the centre of creation.

I can wrap my gift
Carefully.
Put it all together
Fold the paper over and
Tie it up,
Label it and
Give it to You with
Expectation of Your
Surprise and joy: that
You will say
Thank you for my gift of
Pain. For

This year I have only
Myrrh to bring. The
Myrrh of broken lives.
Lives laid waste,
Wantonly wasted,
Bruised and pulled over the
Coals and rubble of
Daily living.

A painful little casket which I
Break over Your body,
Letting flow the
Bitter-sweet odours of

Unwashed bodies
Soiled, sunken minds,
Hearts hemmed in by petrified bone,
Fettered and shuttered spirits.

My gift
Tells of
Myself.

What does it say about
How I think of You? That the
One thing that will give You
Special pleasure is when
I can gather together these
Hurt lives and
Give them to You.
How can I be so certain that
This is what You want, that
This is what You have been
Longing for
Waiting for
Secretly hoping I would give You?

What would I do if I could
Not give them to You?
Knowing that with You I am
Not creating more pain,
But that this is what
Above all You desire, and that You
Love me for
Thinking of
Giving You
Myself.

All that – I am.

HE IS THE IMAGE OF THE UNSEEN GOD
Form us in the likeness of Your image......

16

The seeker and the search

I was told about the star when I was very young. They said that I would see it and I must follow. (I believed them because I could see the pale reflection of the star burning steadily in their lives.) They said that there would be help along the way, but that everyone had their own path to follow, so I must not expect to meet the same people all the time. And sometimes the star would be clouded or obscure, its light darkened, yet strengthened, by uncertainties and doubt, - but seeing was not believing. They said that in the end, following, would be what gave my life most meaning and most depth. And it has been so. I marvel at the source of Wisdom who knew that the journey and the search would be what would captivate us and prove most irresistible.

I know I shall never arrive, not here, but having been and seen and understood I will, like the kings, keep returning home another way.

Infinite and intimate God, You
Compel of me
Questions.
Answers are too finite. They
Do not suit the
Impulse of a
Pilgrim soul. They
Lack the gleam and
Lustre of a
Question, which
Stretches the mind to
Fathom a God, who will
By His very nature, remain
Unfathomable. One who makes
Hungry where most He
Satisfies

HE IS THE IMAGE OF THE UNSEEN GOD
Form us in the likeness of Your image.......

17

The Five Kings

There were five kings of course,
The three who made the journey, and
Found the fourth, lying in a manger. The
Fifth king loitered in the palace.
'Go and find the king and come and tell me, so
I can make homage too,' he said.
But he never made the journey. He
Never intended to. He did not want to
Travel, seek or find. He
Preferred the cloaked corridors of self-made
Power, that careful edifice he had built on the
Sordid cruelty exacted from others. He
Enjoyed the look of fear in the eyes of those who
Scrambled to obey him, the
Humiliation of those who swept the floor,
Washed his feet, or opened their legs.
Those who, in the end,
Stained the streets of Bethlehem with his
Commands, killing, not kings, but
Children.

And what about me?
I see it is not enough to let others
Travel for me. And what if,
What if I, who am so
Skilled in concealment and ambiguity,
Never truly intend to make the journey?

What if a sixth king stalks my heart, a
Jealous Ego-King, rigid with
Arrogance and pride?

Why then I will be left with a
Hunger that snaps and bites at me
Even in my dreams.

Epiphany Conversations

Gold I bring, the
Ecstatic hosanna of a life
Restored. I have survived the
Fire, not quite intact, but with
Worthy scars. My face
Bare before You, I see that
Repair is what I do best.
I would like to
Repair for Your sake all the
Sorrows of the world.

Gratitude, love, these things I have not
Sheltered or kept small for
Safety.
Impossible now to
Love too much. The
Gold I bear is that of
Wisdom.
Make Your ear attentive to
Wisdom. Incline Your heart to
Seeking God. Cry out for
Insight, raise Your voice for
Understanding.
Seek it like silver,
Search for it as
Hidden treasure.
Only then offer the
Gold of Yourself to the
People You meet.

For
You will have a kingdom built of
Mended stones and braided waters,
Softened doors and unhooked gates.
Of patched up roofs of
Reclaimed tiles, salvaged wood,
Refashioned glass. A kingdom peopled by
Doubt-filled, doubtful characters,
All those who have been
Weighed in the balance and found
Wanting.

Frankincense I bring, the fragrant
Dust of being human. I offer the
Examined life, a life of
Silence, prayer, of
Ritual and sacrifice, a life preparing the
Body's capacity to
Abandon itself to the
Cross.
Open Your eyes and see! the
Love of God is within You.
Lift Your face, and behold!
God's face is before Your eyes.
Wait still in the desert for that
Pure moment of exchange from
God's heart to Yours.

For You will be a
Priest among peoples. The
Imprint of God's finger will be
Upon Your shoulder and You will
Kneel before His presence in the
Persons set before You.

For
You will have a kingdom built of
Mended stones and braided waters,
Softened doors and unhooked gates.
Of patched up roofs of
Reclaimed tiles, salvaged wood,
Refashioned glass. A kingdom peopled by
Doubt-filled, doubtful characters,
All those who have been
Weighed in the balance and found
Wanting.

Myrrh I bring.
What kind of person
(Except the fabled wicked witch)
Would give the gift of
Death to a baby at His
Birth? I am a king who has
Fought with dragons and been

HE IS THE IMAGE OF THE UNSEEN GOD
Form us in the likeness of Your image......

19

Beaten. Thrown my
Net over the side and felt it
Break with the weight of fish.
Lived a lifetime of
Joyous mistakes, but experienced that
Swift plunge into disintegration,
Seen hell,
Felt it, breathed it. I

Know what it is to be
Swept away by the river,
Emptied out into the sea and
Drowned in my own brave attempts at
Self-rescue. The
Bruised reed breaks and
Cannot be mended save by the
Devastating onslaught of unexpected
Grace.

I know about
Charcoal fires and
Feeding lambs, the night-time
Crowing of the
Cock. I offer
Myrrh. The whole world needs
Comforting. Why should You not be
the
Balm for people's wounds, the
Hope for fractured
Spirits?

For
You will have a kingdom built of
Mended stones and braided waters,
Softened doors and unhooked gates.
Of patched up roofs of
Reclaimed tiles, salvaged wood,
Refashioned glass. A kingdom peopled by
Doubt-filled, doubtful characters,
All those who have been
Weighed in the balance and found
Wanting.

HE IS THE IMAGE OF THE UNSEEN GOD
Form us in the likeness of Your image......

20

¶ LENT

HE IS THE IMAGE OF THE UNSEEN GOD
Form us in the likeness of Your image . . . . .

21

Towards Easter

I wish to rise from this Lent
Shriven.
Peeled green clean as a
Healing bandage
Clinging to the
Burnt flesh
Pulls away the
Putrefying mess beneath,
Leaving exposed the
Raw
Wound.

Could then my
Naked soul with
Raw intent in
Quick release
Un-fettered
Rise and
Cling with
Lusty lover's lips to
Him who
Gives and gives with
Generous hand.

New sap rising through
New shoots
(from real death to real life)
Kindles,
Flares, bursts into
Incandescent
Flame of
Easter light.

Lenten Grace

It shouldn't have been so.

I had a
Weak, ill disciplined Lent.
Not even worthy to be called
Defiance or rebellion.
It was not that
Colourful. Rather a
Grey lethargy sank on me.
Cold fingers of insidious fog
Crept about my spirit.
Fog-bound, grey, dissolute,
I could not rouse myself,
Enthuse myself with
Disciplines that seemed
Merely to reflect, mimic,
Depressingly, my
Pettiness of mind and spirit.

On Easter Sunday the
Air in church was
Redolent with the heavy scent of
Lilies.
Redolent of death.

But, O my Lord, You came
Running to meet me.
You ran Your hand over my
Face, releasing the slumbering
Images, lifting them out from the
Depths of my life,
Freeing me from a
Tight numbness of heart and soul.
You
Swept me up,
Released me from myself and
Threw me into the air with
Shouts of laughter.

I felt my many layers
Shift and come together as a
Clear glass channel. You
Poured Yourself into me.
Through me swept the
Invigorating water of life.
Down through the
Pit of my stomach and

Out through arms and legs,
Hands, feet.
I felt heart and mind,
Soul and gut
United in singing 'Yes'.
Yes. Lord. Here. Now.

HE IS THE IMAGE OF THE UNSEEN GOD
Form us in the likeness of Your image......

24

Lenten Wilderness

'He was driven by the Spirit
 into the wilderness.'

This time, I too was driven into the
Wilderness. A bleak, cold place. No
Signs pointing the way. No
Features of landscape to
Reassure. The smell of
Fear in my nostrils,
Fear of never being found, of being
Lost for ever, of being by myself
For ever.

Usually I construct various little well-worn
Runways, small disciplines, that
Get me through the
Weeks, like mice through a field.
As long as I stay on them I am
Safe. I can keep my soul occupied, filling
More and more of the world with
Less and less of myself. But

This time I was driven into the
Wilderness, made to step
Off the path and enter the
Wilderness inside myself, to
Remain there, and know how
Lost I am.

The wilderness is not
Prepared ground. It is stony, hard,
Desolate. The cruel sunshine forced itself
Through my wet lashes,
Reminding me of the
Greed for life that put me here. The
Bitter wind soughed mockingly about my
Head as my inflated sense of self
Crumbled and fell about me like
Flakes of ash.

I ran down tunnels in my head until
I was so far away
No-one could reach me.

And yet, and yet, after all this,
I am awaited. This is an
Unlooked for happiness, to be
Awaited. To feel His
Eyes on me still, the
Heat of His hand like
Gold flooding down my back.

HE IS THE IMAGE OF THE UNSEEN GOD
Form us in the likeness of Your image......

25

And some fell among thorns…..

I have found a use for those
Thorns, even though the
Roots stretch back,
Down through the
Years. I
Pull at them,
Shredding my fingers, and
Plait, weaving the
Thick, unwieldy stems into a
Crown.
I've been doing it for months and
Now, now the crown is
Complete.
Dense, dark, heavy,
Stained with my blood,
Perfect. Perfect for
Pressing down on someone's head.

Whom shall I choose?
Well, here's the
Perfect head for the perfect crown.

Fiercely I push it down,
Feel the hair tangle and pull,
Feel the soft skin tear, the
Bone splinter. See the
Trespassing thorns
Draw blood.

I crown You,
King of my shallow, shadow self,
King of all my pain, all my
Months of toil and darkness.

See how I, the
Poorest of Your subjects,
(yet rich because a subject,)
Give You the supremely
Royal gift.
Crowned with my sins of

Despair, You
Cry aloud in Your agonised
Abandonment.

But as for me, at last I am
Free. The ground is
Cleared. Can
Easter sun break through? Will
Easter rain yet shower down my
Parched and thirsty soul?

Even now, You
Smile, as the crown of thorns
Gleams and glistens with budding
Pearls.

Come Apart into the Desert

Once again I hear the call
'Follow me.'
Obedient, I step forward
Into the desert.
Only this time I am
Struck, mired, wildered.
Lost in a
Pathless place.
I stand alone in the dark.
Dry, scaly things rustle and
Threaten with their incessant
Whispering.
Wild winged creatures startle and
Fright at the
Clamour in my soul.

In despair an ancient cry
Rises to my lips.
'Who will push this stone from
Out my soul? I do not want to
Mouth again the hollow hosannas, the
Lifeless protestations of joy,
Sick in my heart that, for me,
The day has not dawned, the
Son has not risen.'

I become in-valid in my misery.
I feel myself come apart,
Disintegrate and fall in flakes of ash.

And then, the moon, the lovely moon,
Escapes the lowering clouds that
Press upon my head and
Hang in chains about my neck, a
Honeyed moon in a milky sky,
Casting a long shadow that
Reaches out and touches my
Empty, weary soul.

My heart thickens with love. I
Turn, and in His eyes I see the
Charcoal fire, the
Flaming crown of thorns.
On my feet the first cold rains of
Spring begin to fall..

HE IS THE IMAGE OF THE UNSEEN GOD
Form us in the likeness of Your image......

27

The Desert

The liminal space of the
Desert, this important, lost,
Essential place, with a sky of
Unattainable stars,
Where I hope to breathe a
Wilder, purer air, have
Space to run and
Chance to sing, where all that is
Intractable, dark, may actually
Begin to
Admit some light, where the
Poisonous serpent, feeding on the
Apples of my
Presumptuous sins, my
Secret superiorities, is caught in a
Fool's paradise, where everything,
Past, present and future is still unfolding, still
Happening, where the
Great detector heart
Calls into existence the
Things that do not exist, where the
Loss that is at the heart of life is
Found.

The Agony

I
Shrink from the knowledge that
All that is of
God in me must be
Put to death. All
Love, all
Gratitude, all
Grace must
Die. And

Shall I
Weep or shout or cry? The
Judas in me plays to the
Christ in me. I try to
Blend, to
Squeeze as much possible out of
You to
Comfort me. But
Stolen water and
Borrowed bread will not do.

God spoke, and the
Word said,
'Let there be dark,' and
There was dark.

This is the stuff of
Blood and sweat and tears.
There will be no
Angel to wipe my
Face, no
Messenger to
Beautify death. What

Soil there is
Erodes and
Slips away, leaving
Bare the
Fruitful land.

HE IS THE IMAGE OF THE UNSEEN GOD
Form us in the likeness of Your image......

29

Jesus and Judas.

Jesus.

I would have liked
Another kiss from you
Today.
(Don't ask why.) A
Kiss coloured with
Intimacy, where all
Hardness and hostility is
Tongued with what is
Soft and articulate, where
You do not feel
Dis-figured by me. For the
Betrayer and the betrayed must
Cooperate in the
Execution. You are
Condemned, for

You will see the
Desire of your life,
Fade away before your eyes, yet

There is no need for the
Tarnished life to be
Thrown to the ground like so many
Pieces of silver. No need for
Another hanging. One
Tree is enough.
This passion will change for ever the
Kiss of death into the
Covenanted kiss of
Life.

Judas.

From beyond the grave,
I too could have wished for
Another kiss. My
Act of transgression, the
Confiscation of
Your life with the
Assertion of my own.
High on the anger born of envy,
Drunk on the
Righteousness of my own fiction, I
Condemned myself,
Not permitting the
Fragile virtue of doubt to
Triumph over the
Destructive capacity of
Certainty.
How could I think to tell the
Son of God what to do? My

Sin – to
Claim your friendship and feel
Afraid. My
Love – impulsive and untidy, so
Partial.

Would it had been a
Life-giving
Kiss of
Consolation.

HE IS THE IMAGE OF THE UNSEEN GOD
Form us in the likeness of Your image......

30

Looking at the Cross

The purple robe has long gone.
They pull away His clothes
Exposing His frail humanity to the
Vulgar gaze. For
That is where we look, at the
Secret hidden maleness of His
Naked human condition.
Did they hit You there too? The
Shame of it. We are
Witnesses to the
Completeness of Your humiliation.
Unable to contemplate the
Pain of the nails, we
Focus on soldiers
Mindlessly playing out our
Greed at the
Foot of the cross.

HE IS THE IMAGE OF THE UNSEEN GOD
Form us in the likeness of Your image . . . . .

31

The Body and the Tomb

He emerges out of the night, this
Private disciple, to do his
Public act of homage. With the
Courage of a father he
Begs for the body. (The vultures shall not
Have their pickings.)

His dearest friend is
Gone, gone, all gone. He

Unhinges the body from the
Rusty pegs. With the
Tenderness born of a
Mother, he
Gathers You together, the
Richness of God's mercy
Heavy in his arms, the healing
Stillness of Your breath
Weeping through the air, for You are
Gone, gone, all gone.

He wraps the fine line of Your
Bruised and bloodied skin in the
Swaddling clothes of death, and
Places the
God of consolation, (who
Consoles us in all our affliction),
Beyond all
Grief and tears,
Sealing You, (my Joy, my
Life, my Love,) in a rough hewn
Cleft of rock. The

Light that lightened the
Gentiles, the
Glory of Your people
Israel, our dearest Lord and
Saviour, now
Gone, gone, all
Gone.

HE IS THE IMAGE OF THE UNSEEN GOD
Form us in the likeness of Your image......

32

¶ THE SEVEN LAST WORDS FROM THE CROSS

HE IS THE IMAGE OF THE UNSEEN GOD
Form us in the likeness of Your image ......

Father, forgive......

Secure within His Father's love He
Asks what only a
Son can ask. He
Calls on what He knows, that the
Dearest quality of
God's love is His
Intense desire to
Forgive.

(God searching for us.
God in love with us.
God reaching out to
Touch us.)

We
Look away,
Shy of partaking in such
Intimacy, -
Son living in the Father
Father living in the Son,

(Nothing you can do can
Ever make Me
Love you less.)

He
Lives in that
Pure moment of
Exchange, from
God's heart to
His heart,
Comforting,
Inspiring and
Full of hope.

(God our God,
Full of grace,
God in Christ,
Full of joy,
Refusing to let our
Sin destroy His
Relationship with us.)

HE IS THE IMAGE OF THE UNSEEN GOD
Form us in the likeness of Your image......

35

Truly I tell you, today...

He breaks the habit of a lifetime
And he asks.
Smash and grab disappear within his
Dis-membered and dis-integrating
Body and mind,
And he asks. He
Understands about need, and,
From the poverty and scarcity of his soul,
He asks. He
Sees Christ, the
One who holds the
Seven stars in His
Right hand, the
Hand that stretches
Pinned and bloody
Toward him on the
Cross and he
Asks, asks for the
Morning star to
Rise within his heart.
'Lord, re-member me.'

And,
Suddenly, the Kingdom
Floods over his head,
Drenching him in the
Giddy, glorious waterfall of
Abundance.

'Today – with me – in Paradise.'

HE IS THE IMAGE OF THE UNSEEN GOD
Form us in the likeness of Your image.......

36

Woman, behold your Son

'Look at me,' He says, 'Woman,
Behold your Son, the
One who grew between your fingers,
Flowed out from between your knees, your
Son, who leaves you to
Seek His Father, whose
Beginning in you is to
Die for you, whose
Cry from the cross
Echoes your own song.
'Holy is His Name.'

Behold your Mother

'Look at her,' He says
'Behold your mother, the
One who says 'Yes' to God,
'Yes' to bearing God's Son,
'Yes' to a sword
Piercing her heart as it
Pierces mine. From her
Womb flows the
Water of life. The
Spirit of God still
Overshadows her. Her
Left hand is
Beneath my head, and with her
Right hand she
Embraces me.

'Look at her,' He says, 'and see
Where she is looking.'

HE IS THE IMAGE OF THE UNSEEN GOD
Form us in the likeness of Your image......

37

My God, My God, why.......

A hollow pit
Yawns in answer. The
Air thickens, grows
Dense and thorny.
Panic stretches and
Tumbles through His
Mind. 'I'm
Losing You. I'm
Losing Myself.
Where are You?'

God unwinds Himself from the
Wood,
Peels Himself away
Strip by strip. He
Empties Himself of
Himself, spilling
Blood and Water.

Nobody else knows He is
Gone, as Jesus
Climbs into the moment,
Not knowing if He will ever
Arrive, ever be able to
Die without God, or
Live again with God.

HE IS THE IMAGE OF THE UNSEEN GOD
Form us in the likeness of Your image.......

38

I thirst

From the cross
Living water
Shouts out 'I
Thirst.' As He hangs,
Dying, living water
Drains from out His
Side, leaving only the
Dark, dank tomb of
Dark humanity in which to
Rest His head. The
Essence of God
Leaks away into the
Ground, watering the
Roots of the
Cross.

HE IS THE IMAGE OF THE UNSEEN GOD
Form us in the likeness of Your image......

39

It is finished

And the
Starry bowl of the sky
Bursts into flames. A
Hot, bruising wind
Scorches the upturned faces.
Suddenly the
Veil of the temple
Rips and roars and we
See, face to face,
God in all His
Terrible majesty.
Spotlights strobe the air
Brightening the
Blackened cross.
God, powerful in a
Bruised and broken Body.
Love, invincible in its
Humiliation and loss.

Death cannot decide the
Boundaries of God's
Love. All we do to
Push God away cannot
Deny Him His
Royal freedom, the
Freedom to be
God with us.

Between the hammer and the nail
Without our aid, God,
Our unknown God,
Forges and
Shapes Himself.

HE IS THE IMAGE OF THE UNSEEN GOD
Form us in the likeness of Your image......

40

Into Thy hands…..

The light flickers and goes out.
Night descends,
Black and unrelenting. A
Thin, wild keening
Strafes the air
Anguish rafts the sky. He
Steps forward
Over the edge of the world to
Return to His Father,
(not knowing if He is there or
not,) and He
Falls, He falls, He falls.
Death grips Him.
All that is God,
All that is human,
Dies. A
Cold, cold absence
Silently screams and scrapes His
Soul.
Stripped, abandoned, alone, He
Sinks down into
Oblivion.

The grain of wheat
Falls and dies.

HE IS THE IMAGE OF THE UNSEEN GOD
Form us in the likeness of Your image…..

41

Love's Rising

He has lain lifeless
All day, all night, His
Sightless eyes watching the
Moon move across the sky. The
Swaddling bands of death
Press His marbled limbs into the
Cold, cold stone. The
Acrid taste of nard,
Aloes, myrrh,
Lingers on His tongue,
Gall and vinegar
Rise within His throat. He
Feels a dark bloom
Growing at His temple and then,

Then the
Electric shock of a
Summons in His ear.
Someone is calling His
Name, insistently
Calling, calling. He wants to
Answer, but He doesn't know
How. He thinks He might be
Lost. The memory of God
Clings and slips through His
Mind, like smoke on water, light on
Fire. The call comes again, and
Again and again.
Close, closer,
Familiar. The voice of
Love, impossible to ignore.

Confusedly He replies
'Here,
I am,
Here I am,
Here I
I am.'

And love,
Lovely love,
Loose-limbed,
Love-laced love,
Light-looped-lingered love,
Longed-for, lately-love,
Leans tenderly over,
Picks Him up and
Holds Him close a
Long, long time against His
Breast, then
Sets Him down and
Lets Him go.

He
Rises up, and
Steps out into a
Morning of
Pure sunshine, the
Freshness of a
Garden.

¶ EASTER

HE IS THE IMAGE OF THE UNSEEN GOD
Form us in the likeness of Your image . . . . . .

43

Easter Dawn

We gathered early, down by the
Water's edge, near the bandstand. I
Watched the river flowing
Swiftly past me.
Patches of debris
Swirled past.
Grass and reeds, tangled round
Lengths of wood,
Fashioned a crude and jagged
Cross. Branches twisted into
Ugly crowns of thorns. A piece of
Sacking, dirty, combat-coloured,
Woven, not torn. A
Dirty polystyrene cup of
Vinegared water.
So many painful reminders.

The swans
Beat up and down, their
Wings clapping like thunder, their
Feet parting the quaking waters.
Moorhens, caught in the wake, frantically
Wagged their heads and
Cried their plaintive, abandoned cry.
So many reminders.

Then, a
Figure emerged out of the
Shadows. A man on a
Bike, a bin bag
Slung over his shoulders,
Pedalled steadily towards us and
Strongly swept up and over the bridge
Across the water and into the
Houses on the hill, his
Dog running before him.

Suddenly a
Blackbird speckled the air with
Song, the
Cherry tree flushed in the
Cool grey light, and our
Hearts, like the dawn,
Rose to meet Him.

HE IS THE IMAGE OF THE UNSEEN GOD
Form us in the likeness of Your image......

45

Easter Surprise

This year, I left the house
Subdued. I wanted to
Feel what *they* felt, that
First time. Like them I
Hurried through the streets in the
Greying dawn,
Sad and downcast by the
Death. My life
Stretched ahead,
Empty, void,
Hungry for love.

The birds were
Mad with chatter in the trees. The
Road sweeper swept noisily. The
Air conditioning from pubs and clubs
Hummed and roared
Pressing against my ears.
I wanted to shout,
'Stop. Be quiet.
Go away. The world has
Stopped. All is ended.'

(All the same, I couldn't
Suppress the
Thrill, the expectation, the
Question.
Will I see Him risen?
Where? Who will show me Him
This year?)

Down by the river it was
Grey too. We sat on
Benches and waited. I
Gazed through the trees to the
Water's edge.
Trees that looked like
Crosses, black etched,
Arms flung wide against the
Pearling sky. The

Shadowed bank on the
Other side gradually moved into an
Intense green. The

Roar of the water over the weir
Thudded in my head. The
Words caught me like fire,
'See yourself as dead to sin and
Alive to God.'

It was then I saw him, the
Litter man, his
Distinctive, green, fluorescent coat
Shining through the
Tarnished dawn light.
(I see him every morning as I
Run round the city walls.)
Is that Him? I thought.
Can that be Him?

I waved, as I always do. He
Looked at me curiously,
Puzzled. A little fearful, he
Peered closer, but he
Did not recognise me in a
Coat. (He only knows me in
Running clothes.) I

Spoke his name,
'Ken'.
Light dawned in his eyes.
Pleasure lit his face and,
In an instant, - in one
Startled instant,
Reflected through his
Frame,
Mirrored in his eyes I
Saw
You, my Risen Lord,

You,
Looking out,
Risen in me.

Easter Morning

We woke early for the
Dawn service in the park.
Even the birds were asleep.
5.30 was actually 4.30 because of the
Cruel placing of British Summer Time.
We stepped out of the house. It was
Raining - quickly back to grab an
Umbrella, - (Jesus might need one, he would not be
Expecting rain). Into the car, then
Back again, - we forgot the
Mobile phone, - and who knows,
God might want to call.
Down the road a quick brush with
White van man, then
Round the one way system
Through the road works,
Surely we are not going to be late,
Surely we will not miss Him?
Park up - oh no, no money for the
Meter. Will we be
Clamped on this morning of all mornings?
Move car, scramble out. It's
Cold. Cram on bobbly hat. Will He
Recognise me in my bobbly hat? I
Fret. Pushing open the gate in the
Greying dawn we
Hesitate. Which way to go?
Where is the place? We
Thread through the myriad paths, the
Scent of the garden strong in our
Faces, the trees rounding out in our
Eyes, the birds stirring now in our
Ears. A figure
Hurries in front of us. We
Follow, the light rain
Dusting our hair. Then we see the
Light burning in the brazier, the
Linen cloths lying
Empty on the ground. The
Clouds open up and the
Sky breaks through like a great
Smile.

HE IS THE IMAGE OF THE UNSEEN GOD
Form us in the likeness of Your image......

47

Resurrection:
To believe or not to believe?
Is that the question?

Daily we hammer God into shape,
Nail Him down with
Carefully crafted, self-made words of
Our determination.

Weekly, we give Him credence,
Slotting into busy lives
Finely calculated, limited acts of
Measured out, scrupulously weighed
Acts of worship.

We love to
Tell God who He is, in our
Earnest intercessions, requesting
(Politely), that He intervene in our
Troubled world, and
Show us that we know Him
As He is.

And then, - then, - in
One tremendous, dazzling leap He
Bursts from out the tomb,
Captivates our hearts,
Shatters our illusions and
Slakes our thirst for
Ever.

HE IS THE IMAGE OF THE UNSEEN GOD
Form us in the likeness of Your image......

48

Easter Carol

Children:
Do you like my nut brown boy
Mister Death? Do you? Do you?

Voice:
The nut brown tent of human clay that
Binds His heart with flesh of mine, the
Walnut skin and polished hair, so
Sweet His kiss, so full of grace, so

All:
I shall follow where He goes,
You shall not say me nay.

Children:
Do you like my green eyed boy
Mister Death? Do you? Do you?

Voice:
He plants a vineyard in my soul, the
Well of life is in its midst, a
Kingdom bright with healing leaves.
Hosannaed palms are riding high, the
Greening seed has yet to die. So

All:
I shall follow where He goes,
You shall not say me nay.

Children:
Do you like my blood red boy
Mister Death? Do you? Do you?

Voice:
The blood red bands of hard pressed thorns that
Bleed and tear His matted head, the
Spittled face and gaping side, the
Shame, derision, mocking scorn, and

All:
Shall I follow where He goes?
You shall not say me nay.

Children.
Do you like my blue black boy
Mister Death? Do you? Do you?

Voice.
The blue black bruising of His skin, the
Cutting cross that scars His back, a
Weight of stones about His neck, the
Rough hewn rock entombing Him, still

All:
I shall follow where He goes,
You shall not say me nay.

Children:
Do you like my snow white boy
Mister Death? Do you? Do you?

Voice:
The snow white lamb who bears my sin, the
Passion of His suffering, the
Tear filled cheeks and sweaty brow, a
Salted sacrifice for me, so

All:
I shall follow where He goes,
You shall not say me nay.

Children.
Do you like my golden boy
Mister Death? Do you? Do you?

Voice.
A golden shore is where He stands, a
Rising Sun above His head.
At His feet a charcoal fire, the
Smell of fish and daily bread.

All:
You shall not have Him,
No, No, No! For
Death is always lost to Love,
Risen from my dust He stands, so
I shall follow where He goes,
You can not say me nay.

HE IS THE IMAGE OF THE UNSEEN GOD
Form us in the likeness of Your image......

50

¶ SAINTS' DAYS AND FEAST DAYS.

HE IS THE IMAGE OF THE UNSEEN GOD
Form us in the likeness of Your image......

A New Pentecost

I saw it from afar. A
Plume of white smoke
Searing and thrusting against the
Grey air.
All around was
Rock and flat and
Dip of weathered peat,
Black and battered stone.
Not fire, I thought, not
Fire, not here.

I drew nearer and saw
Smoke turned to
Spray. The wind was catching the
Downfall*, spreading it in
Far-flung flumes
Twisting and dashing upwards, a
Water of fire.

Laughing, I skipped and
Hopped from rock to
Rock, ducked and
Weaved to escape the
Drenching of that
Smoke. The
Wind caught at my cheeks. They
Flushed and turned to fire.
Fire. The wind
Roaring in my ears
Filled my puppet-like capers with a
Joyful jangle of dance.
Wind. The noises
Racing in my heart made me
Rush to meet
You.

There was no-one to witness.
No-one to tell.
Not like the first twelve who were

Shell-shocked
Out of themselves and into Your
Fire-ridden presence.
Only the silly sheep
Gazed,
Nonchalantly chewing, while I,
Running in flames,
Fell
Headlong into Love.

Abba, Father, tu solus dominus.
Yeshua, Christos, tu solus altissimus.
Mater mea, tu solus spiritus sanctus.

Yes Lord. I am
Here. Send me.

They asked me at home
Where have you been?
What have you done?

The wind-whipped flush of
Fire on my cheeks
Burned anew.

Even so, come Lord Jesus.
Come.

* Kinder Downfall
Peak District National Park

HE IS THE IMAGE OF THE UNSEEN GOD
Form us in the likeness of Your image . . . . . .

53

Trinity

God my mother
Intimately, impartially, concerned for
Me.
God my lover
Passionate and suffering with
Me.
God my friend
Sustaining, reaching out in the
World with
Me.

HE IS THE IMAGE OF THE UNSEEN GOD
Form us in the likeness of Your image......

54

Harvest of Selves

I do not have a sense of
Seasonal harvest anymore.
OK. – the pears hang on the
Pear tree in the garden,
Pendulous and still in the
Quiet autumn air. The
Blackberry scrambles in haste over the
Garden wall, bright black berries
Winking and shining in the
Paling sun. The
Dahlias sigh long yellow petals,
Scattering them like
Tears on the dew-soaked grass.

But I do not have that sense of
Harvest anymore.
That golden image of days long past, of
Ripening corn, of
Trees weighed down with
Burgeoning fruit, of
Grains and crops ripening fast, then
Gathered in and stored in barns, and
Country folk
Singing, dancing and giving thanks.

My harvest is more centred. I
Know about
Abundance. I know about
Gratitude. I know that sense of having
So much that it
Spills over and out. I
Know about the act of being
Picked, and consumed, by someone
Hungrier than I,
Hungry even for my
Bruised, imperfect flesh and
Smudged soul. I
Know that even in the
Act of being consumed I am most
Surely fed, and I
Know how the great
Harvest act of gratitude, of
Gratitude and giving back, makes
Sudden and perfect
Sense of it all.

HE IS THE IMAGE OF THE UNSEEN GOD
Form us in the likeness of Your image ......

55

Annunciation

A hot, hot afternoon.
Dust suspended in the
Sunlit air. A drowsy
Fly, buzzing against the
Half open window.
Distant sounds of children
Playing.
Next door the carpenter's saw
Rasps slowly to and fro.

Across time and years she
Waits, then hears in the
Cradled silence the fine
Tremor of air
Disturbed.

They gaze at each other
Throughout the
Endless afternoon.

Out of the messenger's mouth falls
The Word. She
Inclines her head.
'I am no longer mine but
Yours,' she says.
The Word in her heart
Settles in her womb.

'It's finished,' cries the carpenter,
Hammering in the last few nails.
'Accomplished,' says the maid,
As she feels the sword.

HE IS THE IMAGE OF THE UNSEEN GOD
Form us in the likeness of Your image......

56

St Matthew
and the numbers game

He sees straight through my
Monied mind, peopled as it is with
Countless columns of
Counted coins. I do not
Ask for mercy. I have
Mercy and enough to
Fill the begging bowls of
Those who, from the street,
Cry in righteous
Judgement on us
All.

Fair exchange is no
Robbery I say, but
He did not
Look at me to
Calculate how much I was
Worth. No
Value judgement here. I
Look into His eyes and
See how wholly
Desirable I am. I
Count myself
Lucky to have been so
Found, for the
Sons of Levi have no
Comparative
Offering to make.

He holds out a
Fishing net full of
Holes, calling me into the sheer
Extravagance of God's
Economy. I

Startle up,
Desperate to
Follow.

HE IS THE IMAGE OF THE UNSEEN GOD
Form us in the likeness of Your image . . . . .

57

Thomas, also called Didymus, the twin.

He feels it is test time. He has
Struggled before, all those former little
Brags, (pretending to understand the
Way, the Truth, the Life,)
Now remembered as an outward
Denial of some grievous inner
Doubt, words that somehow put a
Shiny gloss on an anxious inner
Uncertainty, a twin's latent
Readiness for pain.

True to the material into which he was
Born, he has always lived in the
Double-helixed identity of two
Polarities held within one unfolding
Moment. But now, the
Exactness of memory, the
Burning facts of what had happened,
Held him in a misery not felt since
Childhood, his mind filled with a picture of
Damage, of a huge bruise like a black
Sun.

His friends seemed to have forgotten
Everything, nails, wounds, betrayals, even their
Shame. They are busy shouting, in a
Huge collective effort,
'We have seen the Lord!'
He is wounded.
He cannot bear to think he was not there to
See and touch, yet neither can he
Live in a world of forced
Certainty that attempts to liquidate
Doubt.

But then, Christ came and
Looked at him, and
Called him by name. In an
Unforeseen moment of inner transition he
Sees with blinding clarity that, in all his
Diffidence and hesitation to be himself, he is
Accepted, that a complex faith where
Doubt and certainty co-exist can be held
Incredulously and openly.

¶ OTHER POEMS.

HE IS THE IMAGE OF THE UNSEEN GOD
Form us in the likeness of Your image........

59

HE IS THE IMAGE OF THE UNSEEN GOD
Form us in the likeness of Your image......

60

A (foolhardy) Prayer

Come my daughter, I'll
Teach you a prayer.
Here it is.
Lord, since suffering exists
Give it to me, so that
I may
Understand those it
Strikes.
God of my mothers
Throw me into the flames, so that
I may
Emerge at
Peace with myself.
Break me in two, so that
I may become
Whole.
Push me toward
Darkness, so that
I may
Discover your
Hidden face.

HE IS THE IMAGE OF THE UNSEEN GOD
Form us in the likeness of Your image...

61

The Humour of the Gospels

I often wonder
What Jesus laughed about.
Did an irrepressible bubble of
Mirth sweep up inside Him, when He
Looked at the disciples' faces as He
Walked on the water towards them through the
Storm? Did He
Smile mischievously at
Zaccheus' anxious face
Peering through the branches of the
Sycamore? Did He
Grin inside at the simple tricks of
Caesar's coin and the
Woman caught in adultery? Or
Whoop with joy as the
Swine disappeared madly into the
Lake, fling His arms around the
Man restored and
Dance and caper in thrilled
Exhilaration? Did He
Slyly enjoy testing the
Woman at the well,
Teasing and tickling her mind with
Shocking unconventionality? Did He
Relish the wit of
'Who touched Me?' as the crowd
Pressed and thronged about Him, or the
Hidden glee in picking
Ears of corn on the Sabbath, the
Playfulness of riding on a
Donkey? Did He
Pinch His leg to suppress the
Helpless giggles when Peter said,
'Lord let us build three shelters
One for You, one for Moses and one for Elijah.'
Or
Bite His lip to quell the
Sparkling effervescence leaping from His eyes at
Simon's shocked face of outrage as His
Sweaty feet were cleansed and anointed?

And when I leave You, Lord, and
Cross the lake in a huff; when I
Hide in trees, play tricks,
Point the swivel finger or
Disguise myself in thinly veiled
Madness. When I
Prevaricate and conceal myself in
Reasonable argument, or
Reach out to touch You while
Looking the other way. When I
Kick against society or convention,
Posture, pose or
Play the fool. When I
Impetuously bluster or feel
Shocked by someone else's generosity,
Jesus, my Lord, look at me and
Laugh. Laugh with me.

See me as part of Your
Glorious, ridiculous
Creation,
Tenderly comic, yet
Secure enough in Your love to also
Delight in the sheer fun of it all.

A New Beginning

(on handing over walking boots to be resoled)

We have walked
Many a mile together
You and I.
And now,
Now is the time for
You to be handed over to
Another's care. To be
Re-worked,
Re-soled, heeled,
Given a new lease of life.

And when I too stand, in
Penury of soul, will
My Friend
Take me to my
Great Creator? And will
I, be handed over so
Gently? Will my
Beloved companion
Anxiously point out how
Well I have lasted, how
Reliable and comfortable I have been?
How He loves me,
How He has taken care of me,
Cleansed and softened me,
Seeing again the
Scars and bruises brought on by
Years of being
On the Way.
Forgetting (or forgiving) the
Many times I
Tripped and fell.

And will He
Grieve for me,
Knowing the searing pain
That will be mine, as my
Soul is ripped from me,
Torn from my very being in a
Mighty act of Love, the
Awe-ful act of re-creation.

Re-worked,
Re-souled, healed,
Given a lease of New Life.

My dearest Lord, and will You
Come again and
Find me?
As I, with a
Sob of relief
Surrender myself,
Thankful that You are
Faithful, that You have
Come and
Redeemed me.

A Love Song

You've never been in love?
Not once?
Not ever?

My God I love You,
I love You, not because
I have no other, but because
I find within myself no
Separate voice. You
Lay in wait for me.
You cast Your line and
Snared me. Oh
Sweet bond. – I am
Caught so fast that
Hand and foot, mouth, eyes, heart are
All
Bound to You,
Bound to be God, so
Surely caught, so
Surely freed.

It happened in a flash, the
Being ready and the
Pouring in. We spent
Hours, examining each other,
Learning each other by heart. You
Sparked with energy, and it was so
Generous, so powerful a force that its
Overspill was like the
Sun, healing my scars,
Strengthening me,
Warming my bruised bones as we
Fitted
Bone to hollow,
Hollow to bone.
(Let me be entangled in You Lord,
Knotted in Your hair.)

God is Love and so
Lovely is He that
Lovers all
Love Him.

Attachment

A thousand balloons lifted in my heart
Flooding my soul with colour.
Tugging at the strings of my heart they
Lighten my spirit and
Burst out through my eyes in
Crazy kaleidoscopic song.

It is the look of love-
The love that is not mine but Yours.
The warmth that tends my
Fragile bones, soothes and rocks my
Brittle case, frees, melts my
Hardened mask.
The love that is not mine but Yours.

It cannot be contained, this
Warm-rained shower of delight.
How can I not tell You, that
You too, are walking round
Shining like the sun?
How can I not laugh out loud
Openly, in the street, at this
Secret knowledge which I
Hug to myself, this
Secret language which
Runs through me like a hidden
Underground stream. That my
Beloved
Loves me.

To be loved of God is to be
Lovely indeed.

HE IS THE IMAGE OF THE UNSEEN GOD
Form us in the likeness of Your image......

65

Love's Failure

What then destroys
Love? Only this.
Neglect. Not to
Expect You in the face that
Walks towards me, nor
Run to prepare the Way. To
Choose You out of
Habit, not desire. To
Forget You in happiness,
Make use of You in pain. To
Say You are distant and angry and
Deaf to my cry, while turning
Away from the Word I do not want to
Hear. To deny the
Flame was ever lit, the
Promise made, the
Joy felt. To
Say Your name without
Hearing it, to
Assume it is mine to call. Not to
Seek You out in silence, nor
Delight to spend time with You,
Exploring Your face
Breathing in Your smell. To
Grasp my money to myself,
Bow down to riches and power,
Denigrate the poor,
Suppress the knowledge that Your
Saving love is
Shown through poverty,
Humiliation, suffering, pain. To
Jealously demand
Forgiveness and restoration for myself,
Myself alone. To
Preoccupy myself with being
Busy, or even to think that I can
Separate Your work from
My work. To
Want to take a
Holiday from You.

All this a failure, not of
Intelligence, but
Love. For, after all, what
Honour is there in
Denying that I know myself to be
Loved?

Death of a father

He died last night.
Long waited,
Long anticipated.
He'd tried several times this
Past year,
Struggling to push open the door.
This time
The door swung lazily to and fro, on a
Sunlit porch, hardly moving in a
Faint, sweet breeze, - and his
Soul
Slipped through
Unhurried, easily,
Leaving the husk of the house
Silent, bare
Unimportant now.

Where did he go – where arrive?
Was there a sound of
Cheering, of welcome? A sight of
Arms outstretched, of joy and smiles?
The
Scent of new-baked bread and
Wine outpoured, the
Oil of forgiveness
Stirred by the Spirit's breath?

He thought so, and now he knows.
The thoughts and faith that
Sustained him through life,
Surely do not
Disappear at death.

Morning does not vanish before
Noon, nor noon before the
Evening. They
Close up into one. And so
The evening is warm.

HE IS THE IMAGE OF THE UNSEEN GOD
Form us in the likeness of Your image . . . .

67

They knew that they were naked

At the end of the day
Have you ever felt the
Pleasure of
Shedding your clothes,
Dropping them on the floor, or
Folding them neatly on the
Chair, and
Turning
Turning slowly to
Face your love?
Unashamed.
Defenceless.
Have you ever felt the
Warm comfort of
Skin with skin, the
Closeness of an
Unencumbered body, and an
Unencumbered
Spirit?

Build up no
New defences to
Make up for the ones cast off.
Shed the
Meanness of mind and spirit which
Lodge in
Folds of cloth, the
Deceits that
Stow away in pockets like
Loose change, ready to
Jangle and tangle in
Configurations of
Pretence.

Shed the
Bitterness and regrets, the
Tarnished memories that
Cling like smoke.
Discard the
Monotonous and frightening course of
Daily reconstructing yourself as you
Think you
Ought to be,
Reinforcing the frayed seams,
Frantically darning and

Pulling together the
Holes to keep the
Lie from showing.

Throw away your
Existence as a
Succession of costumes, and
Feel yourself
Naked and open,
Ready to receive,
Ready to give.

Spirit of the family

You think that if you
Write me down you will have
Caught me,
Captured (enslaved) me. That at
Last you will
Understand me. But

I am not one to be so
Fixed,
Painted on tablets of stone.
There are more things in
Life than we can
Touch or see.

Every family conceals within itself
Another, - the choice not taken, the
Feeling unexpressed, the
Desire unresolved, or
Pursued down a myriad, myriad
Constellations of ever shifting
Patterns. The

Spirit of the family is the
Art of
Intimate belonging, of
Creative giving. A fragment of
Collective memory which
Lingers as a tantalising fragrance and is
Ever after
Sought. The

Family is where we
Learn to love,
Love ourselves. Where we do not seek
to
Grasp from the
Other the
Value which we
Deny ourselves, (for surely
Nothing makes us more
Vulnerable than loneliness except
Greed.)

Look at your hand. It is the
Hand your parents took for
Safety.

Look at your heart. It is
There the
Faces of the
Newborn,
Recreate the old.

HE IS THE IMAGE OF THE UNSEEN GOD
Form us in the likeness of Your image.......

69

Learning to Love

The beginning of
Love, is to let
Those we love be
Perfectly themselves, not to
Twist them to fit our
Own image.

And so it is with my love for God, and
God's love for
Me.

Even between the
Closest human beings
Infinite distances continue to
Exist. Endeavour to
Love the distance between.
So it becomes possible to
See each other
Whole against the sky.

For so it is with my love for God, and
God's love for
Me.

The
Mystery of God,
Close, entwined about and in my
Heart. The
Mystery of God
Transcendent, whole and perfect,
Unutterably other.

HE IS THE IMAGE OF THE UNSEEN GOD
Form us in the likeness of Your image......

70

JOURNEYING AS A CHILD OF GOD

Teach us to discern your hand in all your works......

¶ ACONCAGUA 2000.

Penitentes
*(ice columns found in the
Argentinean mountains)*

They lean
Silent,
Chiselled by wind,
Bleached by sun into
Attitudes of supplication.
Together they present
Rows of mute
Invocation.
Arms out flung,
Heads bowed, they
Eternally rejoice in their
Suffering stance,
Witnesses to that
Higher grace that they forever
Pursue.

And can my soul
Kneel so still? Can I
Stand the
Harrying wind, the
Merciless sun, the
Continual shaping and
Moulding in my
Search for God?
Can I rejoice in the
Supplicant shape, the silent
Waiting, the watching, so that
At last, I too
Glow in the reflected
Light of the
Setting sun?
.

Dawn

The absolute stillness of dawn.
A mule snuffled, a
Man coughed: the
Wind stirred the tent flap.
I scrambled out,
Stiff and cold and
Stood on a rock
Silent, waiting for that
First ray of sun to
Shower like gold
On my face,
Transforming in an instance my
Darkness to
Light.

Retreat Days

The heat stirs and
Shimmers above the
Rocks. The wind
Lifts
Flurries of dust which
Settle reluctantly
Back on the land.

My soul
Burns and shimmers:
Dry, parched, the
Hot wind
Shifts the dusty film which
Obscures my true desire to
See You more clearly,
Love You more dearly,
Follow You more nearly.

The stars

The stars! The stars!
Realm upon realm of
Galaxies and
Patterns, golden, shining,
Bursting with Your infinite
Mystery.
When I consider Your
Heavens and the
Work of Your fingers …
Can I see You
Hiding in that
Golden curtain,
Your face burning through the
Woven tapestry of
Midnight black and gold?
Looking at me,
Beckoning, calling,
Telling me I have been
Chosen to
Shine too, so that
Others will see and give
You the
Glory.

Return

How to describe
Silent days?
Days where I
Traced and followed an
Inner path.
Moving from the
Dusty plain to the
Ice cold lake.
Each day
Seeing myself more
Clearly; seeing
You reflected in the
Green waters
Looking over my
Shoulder
Laughing and
Wondering with me

¶ ANNAPURNA CIRCUIT

OCTOBER – NOVEMBER 2007

'Namaste,' I

Greet the God
Within you.

Suspension bridges, linking
Land to land,
Earth to sky.
Hanging between and
Hanging over. I
Step off and the
Known world
Shifts beneath my feet.

Bhulbulbe

 - the place where
Water springs from the
Ground. May my heart be
Such a place.

Waterfalls, joyous, abundant,
Leaping from the rock, whether
God is there to
Catch them or
Not.
. . . .

I find myself reducing the
Grandeur of the mountains to a
Manageable scale.
I do the same with God, but
Now, I *know* about His
Grandeur that I cannot
Encompass.
. . . .

'Pine trees take a long time to
Grow,' Silar says.
In my 60th year,
Have I yet started
I wonder.

Paunga Danda

A vast amphitheatre of rock,
Scooped out by God's wind,
Furrowed, furled,
Fluted, whorled,
Majestic in its emptiness.

The scooped out bowl of my
Soul howls with the
Force of Your breath. Your
Cupped hand waits to
Cradle me when at last I am
Empty of myself.

Annapurna

Annapurna, the
Bright, burning snow of
God's eyes
Beaming down upon me.

Annapurna,
Wreathed in clouds
Dancing like veils
Seductively to and fro.
God creeps into my heart,
Rests His cheek against my soul.
'Come and join the dance,'
He says.

Annapurna, God of the Harvest,
Snow laden slopes
Promising heavy crops of
Barley, rice and millet.
Give me this day my
Daily bread, my
Bread of the morrow.

Annapurna, pulling her mantle
Up under her chin, the
Folds and wraps falling in
Crevasses of snow.
Shadowed, luminous glaciers.
God of the mantle,
Wrap me in Yourself I pray
Annapurna flying free,
Elegant peaks
Streaming towards the sun, the
Clear blue of the sky. I
Feel my own sharp edges
Soften and blur. My
Spirit soars to meet You, O my God, as
You
Run to swoop me up in Your
Arms and set me
Flying free.

Annapurna the fortress,
Walled in rock
Flanked by buttresses
Sternly watching our
Little lives far below.
God my rock, my strength, my
Judge.

Manaslu

Strong body, ribbed in rock,
Shoulders of ice.
When my ribs
Weather white and old, will I still
Grow in stature and be
Crowned in snow?

Loss

I lose sight of You, and
Now there is the possibility of
Further loss, forever to be
Glimpsed in
Every other moment. And yet,
Waiting, -
Before You call upon me,
I will say,
Here I am.
My longing for God,
Vast as the sky,
Mysterious as the hidden layers of
Rock. My
Desire as intense as the
Shimmering heat at
Noonday.
. . . .

I swallow the warmth of the day and
Feel You, my God,
Flooding through my
Bleached and dusty soul.
. . . .

God standing on the
Unseen edge of every moment,
Ready to beckon me on.
. . . .

Blood beating in my temples.
God exploding in the
Secret spaces of my heart.
. . . .

The Gangapurna Glacier

A small green lake lies
Trapped below the icefall.
Inch by inch it is
Fed, imperceptibly from the
Forbidding glacier above, and
Overflows in generous rivers below.
So am I fed by God.
So I should overflow in gratitude.
. . . .

The yak's reproachful
Bellow in the night
Echoes in lonely sorrow
Down the valley,
And is answered by
Silence.
Out of the deep I too
Call to You, my God, and
Sometimes there is
Silence.

The sharp, steady rasping of my breath,
Filling the whole of my conscious being.
So vital, and so neglected before.
God, as familiar and ignored as breath.
How often I take You for granted
O my God, not feeling the
Warm, heavy length of You
Constant and sleeping inside me.
. . . .

Deep into the mountains that
Surround me like an
Embrace. A
Shadow amidst the
Greater shadows.
. . . .

Avalanche

The distant
Rumbling of the God I am
Ignorant of –
Dangerous and utterly different in His
Magnitude. The
Mysterious universe of another Presence
Presses round me.

Landslip

Something inside shifted, slipped, then
Shipped itself over the side and
Down the hill. A
Dark, delicious plummeting of
All I have carried so far. I felt
Free, airy, light;
Full of my Self and
Empty of myself,
Knowing about God, and
Knowing God, in the
Instant.
. . . .

I see
Lived-in faces, - faces that are
Inhabited with a
Strange combination of
Wisdom and acceptance.
Is my face lived-in, I wonder.
Who inhabits my face? Does
God make His appearance there?
. . . .

Porters

If I allow them to
Carry my load, how much more should
I be able to ask You to
Carry me, my Christ,
My beloved.
. . . .

Watching snow crunching under my feet,
Full of the sound of my breathing, I
Hear my voice as someone else

Speaking from far away.
But then, in the dazzling brightness, I
Hear the sound of Your voice, and my
Heart is full of a new song.
. . . .

The high, cold desert of the
Dust bowl of the
Kali Gandaki
Rises to meet me. This
Ancient ocean of ammonites. The
Grit laden wind lashes my skin. The
Simplicity of a scarf bound
Tight around my nose and mouth
Reminds me of
Swaddling bands, - bands to
Hold me tight and
Shape me for my future with
God.
. . . .

The eagle brushed lazily past us
Resting on thermals
Intent on other things,
Not suspecting the
Excited thrill that
Ran through all our hearts.
Lifted on the warm breath of Your
Presence, brushing past Your face, I
Remember Your delight in
Me.
. . . .

Walking through the
Deepest valley on earth, the
Kali Gandaki, I
Think of that other valley I have yet to
Encounter, the valley of
Death, and I pray that my
Trust will not falter,
Especially if those
Dearest to me on earth have to
Travel there first
By themselves.
. . . .

Oxen yoked together,
Ploughing the field.
Laughing boys, yoked together,
Carrying water.
Jesus said, 'My yoke is easy. My
Burden light.'
Now I understand, that,
Many years ago, I
Picked up the wrong load. The
Heavy weight of self absorption.
Now the invitation comes again.
'Put it down and
Pick up My lighter load.'
Terrified, I obey.
. . . .

'He has recovered himself,'
Says the guide,
Pointing to Phil.
'But I don't want to
Recover myself,' I think,
'I want to keep
Shedding myself, becoming
Lighter and
Closer to God.'
. . . .

The lesson is learnt early.
Give way to donkeys.
Give way to cows.
'Namaste.'
Bow your head and
Give way to other people.
. . . .

I have stepped into a
Different world and found myself
At home. I still retain the
Vocabularies of protest and doubt, but,
If You would have me be Your slave,
Take me in slavery.
You have stolen my heart. I
Cannot live without You.
. . . .

Thin air extending
Up into clear, blue sky.
Loneliness opening
Inside me like a
Dark flower.
. . . .

The crickets, vibrantly noisy,
Busy being crickets.
The milk-eyed cow, treacle-breathed,
Sombrely chewing grass.
The white vulture
Still as a stone.
All these bring me to wonder
What is the gift God has given
Me, with which I most fully
Respond to the
Call of Christ, and
How can I encourage it to
Grow?
. . . .

Sunrise from Poon Hill.

Dhaulagiri glows and fades.
God is playing His favourite game.
Now you see Me, now you don't. The
Joy in our hearts when he
Appears in His glory. The
Chill when He disappears in cloud.
And yet, through the darkness we
Know that He is near.
. . . . . .
Gratitude for
Everything I have been given.
A strong body and
Glimpses of God. A
New way of seeing.
Always looking
Within what is given for
God's hidden presence. And,
At the last, a
Home to return to.

¶ THOUGHTS FROM CROATIA
(sailing in the Adriatic)

In all this blue and wind I
Remember that I am as
Nothing. I pause at that
Nothingness in gratitude that
God is who He is.
....

Afloat with no address
Where will I call home?
If I have no address I
Cannot be lost. I am
Found in You.
You are my home.
....

God's own pull towards the
Centre of His
Immense deep.
....

It is so easy here to be
All at sea. The
Sweet smell of
Crushed lavender, the
Tanged salt-laden wind,
Nets drying in the evening air, the
Sun sinking below the rim. I am
Peacefully, all at sea,
Curled up in the
Curved wave of God and His
Love for me.
....

That wild sensation of
Speed and danger, and the
Way we all fit into an
Ideal whole,
Sea, sun, wind, sky.
....

The hillsides covered with
Racing cloud shadows.
God racing through my heart.
....

Lightning tears the sky at the
World's rim, letting in
Torrents of God's love and mercy.
....

The Kornati Archipelago.

You trace the curve of my
Spine with Your thumb, each
Knob explored for its
Human boniness.
Whenever I am away, You
Draw me back.
....

God becomes His own geography.
God at the centre of my world.
God, the great I am, marks
The Way, with neither
Beginning nor
End.
....

God passing by in the
Ecstatic pirouette of the
Tornado,
Sucks the air out of my sails,
Spins me round and
Lets me go.
....

It is enough today if
Where I am
God is found and
Loved and praised.
....

Failure and the concealment of
Failure,
Bones darkening and shattering,
Bruises that rise and disappear.

All turns to sawdust in the
Inside of a breath, my
Relationship with the profound
Taken away by the lie, with
No hope of retrieval.

And then I lie down and let the
Sheets drain the heat from my body.
Before the sky within is fully dark as when
Night ebbs into the ground, I
Sleep. Windows open here and there
onto
Deep and purple galleries, and
Christ walks again in my heart.
. . . .

The anchor falls as
Heavy chains drop from my heart.
Shadows come and go in the
Hollow of Your cheeks as
Wind chasing clouds across the sky.
Hair tousled by the wind
Smelling of the sea, I feel
Your breath fall on the
Back of my neck.
The air liquid clear, the
Water airy as sunlight.
. . . .

Every day, every moment, spent
Working out where in the
Whole entire sea I am.
Laterals, cardinals, markers buoys,
Lighthouses, rocks, islands, shoals,
Using compass, bearings, dividers,
Sun and wind,
Time and space collapse into the one
Present moment.
Free from earth bound preoccupations
Under the blunt sky, not
Floating aimlessly but
Liberated from the
Poisonous urge to control.
. . . .

Mooring buoys.

I come alongside You,
Head to wind, and try to
Catch You with the boat hook of my
Expectations. But You
Float away on a tide of
Silence.

It takes many trials for me to
Realise that I must
Come alongside and
Wait in silence for
You to drift onto me.
I do not need to
Snatch at You, or
Corner You with my
Frantic demands to be
Loved.
. . . .

Fix your eyes on the
Far distance and
Everything else
Falls into place.
. . . .

Intermittent rolls of thunder.
God clearing His throat,
Reminding us of His Presence.
. . . .

Each island unlike any other and
Perfect in Your sight.
Each wave and cloud and fish
Unlike any other and
Perfect in Your sight.
Each person, unique and individual,
No one else, in quite the same way ever
Did or ever will
Imitate You in quite the same way.
. . . .

Where do I stop and the air begin?
In the sea, where is the
Dividing line between
My skin and the water?
In the wind, where does

JOURNEYING AS A CHILD OF GOD
Teach us to discern your hand in all your works . . . . . .

86

My breath cease and
Yours take over?
The tension in the rope, and the
Tightness in my fingers, I
Hold on to what I have of You.
. . . .

Sitting on the jagged limestone cliff
Over head seagulls
Wheel and plunge
Crying loudly. You reach down and
Steal my heart. The
Sun climbing high and hot in the sky
Returns Your embrace
Reaching out its arms to You.
. . . .

The sun baked down, the
Breeze stirred in brief, hot gusts, the
Sky became a burning pale yellow, the
Sea a shimmering rim of gold. The
Sails flapped idly, the
Boat slapped the water
Rhythmically up and down. I
Watched the world dissolve and melt into
Your great Goodness.
. . . .

I thread the ropes round and over as
You thread Your fingers
Through my hair.
. . . .

Thunder, and the air
Crackles between God and me.
God, not to be contained
Overflows through the clouds,
Justice which does not rely on
Counting or weighing,
Mercy which has nothing to do with any
Law we make.
. . . .

White limestone hills
Lozenges in a turquoise sea.
Grey and green scrub of grass
Lifting thistled heads to the sky.
. . . .

The world turned out to be
Blue, rushing and sparkling,
Water and sky,
Swaying, rippling, flashing
Blue.
. . . .

Lightning strikes the night sky,
Thunder growls and prowls,
Splits the hills.
God in all His authority and majesty
Huge and mysterious
Passes through our midst.
Life moving beyond our reasoning,
God, with feet in eternity,
Plays and diverts Himself in the
Skies of His creation.
. . . .

Lightning and thunder
Beat in my very blood. A
Cosmic dance.
Everything shifted under the
Golden wash of the sky.
I am in a
Different place where I have to
Think differently and find myself a
New way of being.
. . . .

You call to me to
Sink from the shallows where I dwell into
the
Immense blue depths of Yourself.
You are awake in the sun,
Asleep in the sea,
Travelling in the wind I
Hear Your song in the sails.
. . . .

Rowing back on the darkened sea You
Take me out of my depth. All my
Chattering misapprehensions
All the
Wearisome detail I
Burden You with, all
Cast overboard.
. . . .

You tug and tug at the
Ropes of my heart and I feel the
Knots of my soul
Loosen, weaken. I am
Unravelled, straightened out.
I become a
Useful piece of string once more.
....

A Trinity of
Sky, sea, wind. The
Infinite dome of the creator sky. The
Cradling servant sea. The
Freshening wind of change
Rising and blowing
Where it will.
Within me
....

God says, 'There is
No-one with whom I would rather
Spend the days than you.' And I
Love Him more and more for
Knowing He says that to
Every other person as well.
....

God awakening in the
Depths of my soul. I am
Empty and therefore lack
Nothing.
I am
Absorbed by the same
Dark gaze that came on
Annapurna. You are so
Familiar and yet so
New to me each day.
....

Marked by forgetfulness, the
Number of loss and the
Vast light stands still. A
Katabatic wind
Falls down the mountainside, the
Rain falls and falls. The
Swell of the heavy sea threatens to

Drown me in a chill of
Separation.
....

Your voice reaches me through the
Sea, the sun, the wind, not
Diluted or filtered but
Fresh, immediate, alive,
Living.
....

The bird sits still watching
God at work in His world.
The dolphin dives, joining
God at play in His world
I breathe, waiting with
God in His world..
....

Today, a sign of God's
Mercy in the world, as
Wide as the sea.
....

I trespass the seas and
Islands of my mind,
Setting a course, a
New alignment with God.
Finding myself in relation to my
True north, all else
Falls into perspective.
....

Dubrovnik.

If my life is spent in
Glad expense for You, then
There will be
No need for castle walls or
Ramparts, neither will I have the
Sorrow of knowing that I am
Keeping myself apart, living
Outside of You.

¶ CANALS AND RIVERS 2008.

On the waterways endeavouring to
Spend my life as pilgrim. How
Stressful it is to go at another's
Speed. What
Duress at having someone go
Past just as I am setting off. How
Tiresome to have to
Wait for someone else to
Saunter by.
....

When entering the tunnel of
Darkness, keep within the profile of
God in order to escape the
Worst of the bruises and
Scrapes along the Way.
....

It is so easy to come adrift,
Unpinned from the very
Moorings that we thought to hold us
Safe.
....

The beauty and pain of the world. A
Moth speckled black and white, wings
Folded as in prayer, offers a deathly
Orison of praise to its
Creator, lifeless on the lock gate.
....

Even a broken reflection mirrors the
Perfection of the One above.
Windswept water borrows some
Beauty from the Owner.
Fragmented light plays with the
Personality of the Whole.
Indoor light may imitate
Outdoor light.
....

For a time the drizzle is
Cool, refreshing even, a
Faint breeze blowing on my

Face. Then a grey
Dampness creeps into my
Soul and Your
Absence seems too enduring to
Bear.

Raising the paddles of my heart
God's love comes
Surging, rushing in,
Threatening to overwhelm and
Drown.

Only when the level of God's love has
Filled the empty lock of my
Heart, have I the means to
Push open the gate and
Go out to
Meet the world.
....

Mooring.

It's a shame if my heart bears a sign saying
Private Property
No Mooring, - (no
Not even overnight.)
Visitors Keep Out.
Who knows what
Help I might have been to someone
Helplessly floating by,
Caught up on the rising waters of
Sorrow?

This sign warns.
Overnight Mooring Here.- Yes,
Here! But we'll make you
Pay. You'll
Pay for it if you
Moor up here.
Is my soul a manicured lawn
Setting up a

Slippery slope, not to be
Accessed? Or a root-strewn, rushy bed,
Padded with water lilies, where
Maybe God could tie up and
Take His rest?
……..

Birds.

Canada geese
Plump and self assured,
Scavengers all,
Moving in a crowd
Anonymous together. The
Feral marauders of the
Waterways.

The heron stands
Aloof, self-sufficient,
Nervously eyeing us up,
Frighting at the least
Forward gesture.

The grebe, poised, aware,
Dives into its private space.
Nine, ten seconds, before it
Confidently lifts its head to the surface.

The swan, demure, seductive,
Sidles up sideways, then
Hisses in attack.

Ducks scatter and
Squawk in a flurry of
Splashes.
Moorhens nervously
Bob their way past. The
Blue zip of the
Kingfisher pulls us after him.

You come to me as a
Rare bird, the bloom of
Apricots about Your
Skin, the scent of
Peaches in Your
Hair, beautiful to behold.
……………
You listen in to my
Thoughts, my questions, my
Meanderings, and You
Smile as You remind me
You are not an
Object to be understood, but a
Mystery to be
Loved.
………..

I looked through the
I of me into the water,
Stepped over the walled garden of my
Self and drowned.
…………..

I wake and sense a
Distance separating us, an
Intolerable distance keeping us
Apart as effectively as a wide
River in flood. I am full of
Trouble, so uncertain.
Stupid to think I can
Entice You back to a
Terrestrial garden of
Happiness. How can that brief
Bubble of joy disappear, go so quickly
Flat, finished, dead? I
Reach out to touch the
Gloom hovering about me and
Withdraw a hand
Damp with despair. It is
Bad enough not to
Find You, but even the

Search is now
De-spiriting my soul. The
Thought that You are
There, but I will
Never find You. You are not to be
Mine. The yearning to be
Chosen, to be brought into
Existence, cannot be quenched without
Destroying the one who
Desires.
....

Is it better to know that
You are there, - You still
Live, but I will never
See You again, or to
Know that You are
Not there, have
Never been there, and
Cannot be found ever again?
....

I woke up and You
Weren't there. The
Sheets were tidy, not
Rumpled, crumpled or
Shaped around You. I
Listened and could not
Hear You.
Desolation swept my heart.
Another day without You
Pressed its sadness through me.
....

Outside in a drenched world
Rain draws off into a
Purpled sky.
Green comes out, sharp, chilly,
Wet, delicious.
....

Sunday church on the waterways.

Can it be that my
Eagerness to please becomes an
Embarrassment? There is a
Rebellion against having to
Listen, being
Forced to echo, out of a sense of
Duty, these
Meaningless ditties. Surely the
Desperation shows in my eyes? In a
Dampness of mild shame I
Withdraw slightly into another
Shade of self. But

God gazes at me beneath
Arched eyebrows, looking
Amused and alarmed at the same time. Then
Speaks with a gentle, easy, brief
Eloquence, the skeletal form of His
Suffering, glowing like
Naked bone.
I am but a beginner in the
Language and meaning of Your
Love. Most painful of all is to recognise a
Passion greater than my own.
All that occurs is an
Exposure of Your
Tenderness.
....

I dread the loneliness I face without You, the
Inertia, the boredom, the
Senselessness of unmeaning.
I will die just because it is
Winter. I gaze into the
Murky evening light
Invaded by a fluttering crowd of
Vagrant mosquitoes, the place
Deserted now and
Empty except for
Ourselves.
....

I seem to set the questions and yet still
Fail to find the answers. Almost
Everything I see and smell is
Recognisable, though there is
Nothing to report save what is
Invisible and unmistakeable.
Redemption is an exercise in
Conviction, with its own
Reality.
When You come again, will You find me
Changed, changed with
Thinking about You?
. . . .

I clutch at You,
Terrified You will
Disintegrate under my
Clumsy fingers. The
Nervous inroads of
Hunger gnaw
Ceaselessly.
. . . .

Something of God is
Shadowed when I choose
Evil.
. . . .

I wear myself out
Travelling from
Misery to boredom, to
Resignation and back.
. . . .

Evil caught me
Avoiding his eye, so he
Approached me directly. He
Slid his fingers into my
Tongue, grasped me by the
Throat and spilled the
Loitering words into the air.

'I never meant to do it but you
Wouldn't listen.'

The words hung there,
Full of falsity and fault,
Staining the air with their
Poisonous taste.
I caught Evil's eye
Over your shoulder.
Grinning he departed
. . . .

Seven million starlings
Detonated out of the sky
Wheeled and circled,
Circled and wheeled,
Orbiting the field,
Elasticating longer, twice
Winging shorter, three times
Vanishing over the hill,
Back, perfect in flight
Perfect with each other.
. . . .

I trace the
Bare outlines of His
Eyebrows, the
Warm crook of His
Elbow.
. . . .

Out of the depths O God I
Cry to You.
When I think I am
Protecting myself I can be
Struggling against my
Rescue.
. . . .

The waters never
Parted for him, not
Once in his
Whole life.
. . . .

I don't have to
Force some theory on a
Mystery and make some
Foolishness out of it.
. . . .

A vapour trail
Gashes the sky which
Heals itself,
Quietly, without fuss or
Rancour.
. . . .

Walking along You
Wind Your arm around my
Waist. God, beguiling, generous,
Life enhancing, returns to me,
Gathers me together with
Hungry and heedless forgiveness,
Delighting in the rebirth of my love.
This is what I came back for. To be
Loved like this. Strange to find that by
Merely arriving, I create so much
Pleasure.
. . . .

Section 3:

¶SNAPSHOTS
and your likeness in all your children......

HE IS THE IMAGE OF THE UNSEEN GOD
Form us in the likeness of your image......

Draw Yourself

(in the therapeutic process each of the snapshot children will have been asked to draw themselves)

God draws Himself with infinite
Care and thought.
He places Himself, the baby, in a
Crude, splintery
Feeding trough, for animals.
The walls behind are
Blackened, murky, yet
Illuminated by an
Intense light that
Streams from round His
Head. His mother
Watches. His father
Waits. He Himself is
Bound tight, held in
Straps of swaddling cloth.
It is very still.
It seems as if the world too
Watches, waits and listens.

What does it mean?
What does it tell?

God, as baby,
Pulls me to Himself.
He is not helpless.
(No baby is helpless.) He
Makes me draw near and
Look at Him
Closely. His bright light
Illumines my face. My face
Shines with His light.
He sees me.
I see him. He
Stirs a great surge of
Love that makes me want to
Shout and sing and laugh and cry.

It was for this that
He was born, and that
I was born.

God called His drawing
'This is my body, - given for you.'

Paradox 1

To live can be a
Denial of life.
To live can be a
Denial of death.
Fear only that
Life which does not
Spring from
Death.

Paradox 2

Where does thought come from?
Where did it hide before
Entering my head?

Who will forgive me?
Who will forgive Abraham the
Death of his son, or
Hermione the loss of
Herself?
Yet who can
Find what they have
Not, already,
Lost?

Truant

I spend my life
Running, from
One distraction to
Another.
Filling my life with little
Sins. Choosing insipid acts to
Pass away
Time. Without
Bothering to
Find out
Who,
Who is doing the
Choosing?

HE IS THE IMAGE OF THE UNSEEN GOD
Form us in the likeness of Your Image......

97

Desmond (8)

I circle his
Thrashing body with
Tight arms. He
Flails, jerks,
Intent on
Escape.
Sweating, he
Digs with
Sharp elbows, but his
Heart is not in it.
He is not
Committed to
Freedom. He has always
Confused
Love and abuse.
I feel his
Fake resistance, his
Snuggling up to my
Bruised body, and
My heart
Contracts with
Love, pain, the
Pity of it all.

HE IS THE IMAGE OF THE UNSEEN GOD
Form us in the likeness of Your image......

98

Timmy, crazy Timmy (6)

I liked it when I had the
Injection. I was happy.
It's easier to think about
Pain in my body than
Pain in my heart and mind.

I am in a car.
I am invisible.
When I get home Mum
Gives me some food.
I come alive.
I am a boy.
I like being a boy.

I need a boat to get me through the storm.
There will be a lot of rain and
Big waves, but it will not sink. A
Big wave comes and my Mum is drowning.
I dive in and get her. In
Real life I can't save her. In
Real life I shout for help.

We had a cat. It kept eating
Sloppy poos, so Mum took it to the
Park and left it.
When I am naughty Mum takes me to the
Children's home and
Leaves me.

I dream at night of a man on
Top of the cupboard. I
Get out of bed to
Get the man to play. A
Ghost comes along. He
Eats the man. I put the
Pillow over my head.

They say:'
If you had the choice
Where would you like to live?'
'How do I know?' says Timmy.
'

How can I tell?'
Poor Timmy. Crazy Timmy.
All-at-sea Timmy.

Timmy. Leaving

His face darkened,
His eyes brightened with
Anger. Nothing soft here.
Sharp, uncomfortable, he
Searches for a place of
Rest. But there is no
Refuge in this night. No
Intimacy that warms or
Satisfies. He
Flings himself on a round of
Ceaseless, impulsive
Activity, to explain the
Smoke that
Pours out of him,
Blackening his face.

Now, face down, he
Hunts himself for
Errors, walking barefoot through the
Flinty interior of his mind.

He sees his life as an
Empty cardboard box,
Overturned by the side of the
Road, with
Nobody in it.

He lives with the
Fear that he will one day be
Seen through and
Ultimately,
Eternally
Discarded.

HE IS THE IMAGE OF THE UNSEEN GOD
Form us in the likeness of Your image . . . . .

99

Keith (7)

Keith swaggers in
Chocolate eyes agleam with
Pride. Memories? - oh yeah
What do you want?
The time I
Stole a milk float
Set fire to the school
Killed the rabbit
Knocked down the neighbour?
No? What then? - the first?
Oh the first, - first is -
When - I feel it now -
Squeezed ....

The first memory.
Squeezed under his mother's arm, he
Feels her fear as she
Runs, clutching him tight,
Through the back door, his
Father bursting through the
Front, intent on damage, intent on
Damaging
Her.

Now he sits at night
Frozen on the stair
Watching, listening,
He sees the door chain
Rattle. He hears a
Knocking.
Sleepless he
Waits, and waits and
Waits.

This waiting is too
Desolate, too
Frightening. Better to
Frighten than to be
Frightened.
So
Who can I hit now?

HE IS THE IMAGE OF THE UNSEEN GOD
Form us in the likeness of Your image ......

100

Ali and the laugh (10)

The man comes into the room.
He draws the curtains.
It is dark.
The man is in the shadows.
His shirt is undone.
His zip is undone.
He rips Ali's clothes off.

Afterwards Ali is on the floor in the
Corner. He is
Crying and hurt.
He can hear the man laughing.
The laugh is cruel, the laugh of
Someone who has done something
Wicked and cruel to
Someone small and helpless.

Ali knows what the man has done is
Wrong. He doesn't tell
Anyone. He is
Frightened.

The man stands over Ali and
Taunts him.
'How can your mother help you now?
If you tell your mother I'll
Say you made it up.
No-one will believe you.
How can your mother save you?

This is as bad for Ali as the
Rape.

HE IS THE IMAGE OF THE UNSEEN GOD
Form us in the likeness of Your image . . . . . .

101

Simon (7)

Am I the same as my Dad?
(I have seen my Dad slap my Mum).
Am I the same as my Dad?
(My Dad went to jail).
Am I the same as my Dad?
My Dad lived on a boat.
One day we went to the boat.
It had gone. We searched for three days.
I was crying.
Am I the same as my Dad?
(Dad has disappeared).

It's like a busy road inside my head.
Red cars going up
Blue cars going down.
People walking at the side.
Busy, dangerous, crowded.
No room for mistakes
(You'll get caught and punished).
No time to rest
No space to breathe.
Was it like this for my Dad?
Am I the same as my Dad?
Where is he?

HE IS THE IMAGE OF THE UNSEEN GOD
Form us in the likeness of Your image......

102

Kristy (8)

I remember Dad. He took me
Roller skating. We went on the swings.
Dad died on the 14th October 1997.
I was six years old.
I was six years old when he started to
Lay into me. It was very painful and I didn't
Like it much. He also put his
Big willy into my
Front bottom.
Mum was there.
They made me watch them having sex,
On the settee, on the floor, in the hall
On the bed.

Dad died in prison.
He hung himself.
He went to prison because of me.
Mum has gone away.
I live somewhere else.

The worst thing is
How can my Mum
Forget she has a
Daughter?

HE IS THE IMAGE OF THE UNSEEN GOD
Form us in the likeness of Your image . . .

103

Lena (7)

In school
Kids are nasty to me.
They hit me.
They call me names.
Mum says
'Hit them back if they
Hit you first.'
So I do.
I get into
Big trouble.

I have a dog called
Buster. I hold up his
Rubber bone. He jumps for it.
We have fun together.
I like Buster.
Buster likes me.

My biggest trouble is

Does my Mum like me?.... (I don't think so).
Do I like my Mum?...... (I don't know).

HE IS THE IMAGE OF THE UNSEEN GOD
Form us in the likeness of Your image......

104

David (8)

He looks, wide boy blue eyed
Suspicious, veiled.
What he has seen cannot be
Revealed. A father
Drunk and loud
Beating with flailing fists and feet his
Mum, and he on the
Bed between them.

Now he too beats his Mum.
At eight years old he
Lashes out in a fury of
Anger. Rage at himself for not
Protecting his Mum.
Rage at her for not protecting
Him.

HE IS THE IMAGE OF THE UNSEEN GOD
Form us in the likeness of Your image.......

105

James (4)

He broke my legs when I was
Six months old.
He bruised my eyes when I was
One year old.
He beat me round the mouth and
Split my head when I was
Two years old.

Now I am four years old and a man.
Now I attack myself.
I scratch my arms.
I mark my skin. I
Run wildly into the road and
Bite and kick anyone,
Anyone who comes near.
I might as well.
It's obvious.
My life tells me that for me
Love does not exist.
I might as well
Destroy myself in the ways I have been taught.

James (4)

I gave him my
Pencil case to
Look after, while I
Talked with his
Mum and step Dad.
Solemnly he
Pressed up against my
Knees. He
Sharpened each pencil until it
Broke, then started
Again, and again, and
Again. He showed that he
Knew what it was, to be
Brought to
Breaking point.
He showed me his
Need to be mended.

HE IS THE IMAGE OF THE UNSEEN GOD
Form us in the likeness of Your image.......

106

Basil (7)

My Dad came
Rushing at my Mum,
Fists out
Full tilt.
She
Side-stepped. His
Clenched fists went
Through the fish tank.
Blood streamed down his arms.
He came and lay down on
My mattress on the floor.
He wanted to
Die.

I
Dialled
999. The fish
Died anyway.

Next time she
Side-stepped, he got
Me. His fists
Hurled me down the stairs.
Blood streamed down my
Head and back.

I still
Dialled
999, but
Something, a
Spark, even as it flared,
Died in me.

Now I throw over chairs. I
Lob bricks. I
Run and jump and
Set off alarms. I

Dial
999,

Anything to try and
Ignite the spark,
Keep it flaring
Signalling my need
My turmoil
My imminent death.

HE IS THE IMAGE OF THE UNSEEN GOD
Form us in the likeness of Your image......

107

Darren (9)

I just want to hurt somebody because
My Mum hurts me.
She jumps on my back and
Hits me.
She can't control her temper. She
Strangles me and
Pins me to the floor while she
Hits me.
Grandma used to do it to her kids, so
Now my Mum does it to me.
All my auntie's house
Have got a bad temper, but
My Mum is worst than theirs.
I don't want to have kids because I'm
Scared of doing it to them.

I want to live with my Dad, but
I found out he went to prison for
Selling drugs.
I've only seen my Dad
Once this year.

My auntie Julie says there is
Something wrong with me and then
Expects me to be her friend.

I don't want to ever go home to my Mum. She's
Ripped childline and
Other kid's numbers
Out of the book so I
Can't phone them.

We make excuses for the
Bruises, if
Anyone
Asks
Where they are from.

HE IS THE IMAGE OF THE UNSEEN GOD
Form us in the likeness of Your image......

108

Grace (2)

I withdraw into silence and
Gaze out at a world which
Whirls past me so
Fast that I have to
Steady myself by
Freezing.

Motionless I monitor my breath.
Perhaps if I do not breathe the
Thief will not notice me. He will
Pass me by for another. But I cannot
Not breathe for ever. So when my
Breath comes again, it comes
Fast and furious,
Hotly expelled in howls of rage and fear. I
Make as much noise as I can so that
You will see the thief and
Rescue me.

Don't leave me.
Save me from the
Terrors that fly by night, the
Pestilence that strikes at noon-day, those
Horrors that are yet preferable to
Acknowledging that I have a
Mum I can see and touch, but who is
Forever
Out of reach.

HE IS THE IMAGE OF THE UNSEEN GOD
Form us in the likeness of Your image . . .

109

John (9) and ADHD

There was a picture in the
Tate Modern, of
Three people
Standing on a balcony
Gazing, with their backs to me, at
Something.
Curious, I drew near to
See, see what
They saw.

I saw a figure,
And,
For one split second, did not
Recognise
Myself.
(The picture was a mirror.)

Is this how John lives?
Does he live in that
Eternal
Split second,
Forever outside
Looking in,
Seeing, yet not seeing,
Uncomfortable, because it is
Familiar, yet unrecognised?

He has a strange
Dispassionate view,
Coldly curious.
He thinks he knows himself, and then he
Experiences that he doesn't.
He is confused by the world that he
Senses has a
Pattern, but where the
Pattern that is himself has
No place.

John and protest

He sits
Staring at the table,
In a state of
Permanent protest.
Resentment curdles on his face,
Resentment at his Mum's
Care-less anxiety that brings him
Here, yet which blows
Wafer thin, out through the doors of
Other concerns.
His voice thins with anger and
Slips unbidden from his throat.
Ice-cold heat strains through his
Eyes, as his
Forbidden self
Dulls into submission. He is
Crushed, un-easy with
Himself, unsettled by a
Tangled confusion that leaves him
Forever wrestling,
Self upon self.

Mikey (10)

I'm a joker, -
Well
Life's a joke isn't it?
It has to be.
It has to be, to quell the
Queasy trepidation that might
Otherwise
Rise up in great
Waves of vomit as I
Vehemently reject
All that I have lost,
All that I pretend to laugh at.

These I have lost.

My place as
First-born, gone,
Taken by a sister who
Died in her cot.
My Mum leaving me in her grief.

My Dad
Beating my Mum.
My Mum
Leaving my Dad,
(But not joining me).
My Mum leaving me in her pain.

My new Dad who
Competes unfairly with me for my Mum.
(How can I hit him when he's ill?)
My Mum leaving me in her joy.

Their new baby, a
Love child,
(Whom I love bitterly too).
My Mum leaving me in her heart.

I jealously hug my
Losses to myself in a
Rash, a rush of
Rage.

You have to laugh.
Well –
I can't cry can I?
Big boys don't.

HE IS THE IMAGE OF THE UNSEEN GOD
Form us in the likeness of Your image . . .

111

The Trap

Carole's Mum

You have to understand that I went to
Hospital and
Had
Two babies, but I only came home With
One – and he is
Damaged. Was I careless? Was I at
Fault? Was there something I didn't See or
Feel or understand?

Now I live in a
Panic of protection – I know I do.
I see
Evil lurking at every door
Waiting, watching to
Snatch my children away,
Dispose of them
Strip them from my side,
Leave me gasping, winded,
Bereft,
Inconsolable,
Rocking and heaving
Disintegrating in black waters that
Close above my head.

Carole (6)

Well obviously I
Shout and tease and annoy. I
Have to, to remain
Separate. My Mum would
Gobble me up otherwise,
Consume me, to
Keep me safe. If I got too
Close, she might
Fall on me,
Crush me, so she could
Breathe me in like
Dust, absorb me into
Herself.

It's crazy the
Clamour I make, the clamour designed
To
Keep her away and keep her together. I
Need her you see. It's
Confusing, but I know that the
Noise that is me will both
Push her away and reel her in.
This is my allotted task, the
Job I've been given to do. (To
Unreel the spool of bonding that is also
Bondage).

If you take it away from me I'll
Disappear, I'll
Break in pieces,
Break apart in little pieces on the
Floor, so scattered and
Destroyed that I'll
Never,
Never get mended again.

HE IS THE IMAGE OF THE UNSEEN GOD
Form us in the likeness of Your image.....

112

Danny (10)

The thing is, I only have to
Think of him and my insides turn to
Water, shifting and gurgling,
Erupting,
Pouring out of me in
Torrents of shit.
The
Stench, the colour
Disgusts me, fills me with
Self-disgust, self-
Loathing. I

Couldn't protect her
Then, and I can't now. I
Grab the shit in a fury and
Smear it over the
Walls, press and squeeze it into my
Clothes
Painting a
Brown and filthy picture of the
Shit that is me. I

Hammer the walls with
Bruised knuckles,
Shouting aloud my
Fear and impotence, my
Knowledge that I am
Less than a
Man.

HE IS THE IMAGE OF THE UNSEEN GOD
Form us in the likeness of Your image . . . .

113

Louis (7)

Louis Tinn, Louis Tinn,
Has no Mum,
What's wrong with him
Louis Tinn?

Louis Tinn, Louis Tinn,
Has a Mum, she's drunk on gin,
What's wrong with him,
Louis Tinn?

Louis Tinn, Louis Tinn,
Has a Mum on heroin,
What's wrong with him,
Louis Tinn?

Louis Tinn, Louis Tinn,
Lives with Nan, she's tired of him,
What's wrong with him,
Louis Tinn?

Louis Tinn, Louis Tinn,
He's bad at school,
What's wrong with him,
Louis Tinn?

Louis Tinn, Louis Tinn,
Can't read or write or dance or sing,
What's wrong with him,
Louis Tinn?

Louis Tinn, Louis Tinn,
Knows what's wrong,
What's wrong with him,
Louis Tinn.

Louis Tinn, Louis Tinn,
Is like his Dad, and full of sin,
That's wrong with him,
Louis Tinn.

Louis Tinn, Louis Tinn,
What to do with Louis Tinn?
No-one loves him,
Louis Tinn.

And Louis Tinn knows.

Miles (8)

Swollen with words and feelings he cannot
Identify, but which
Spill over in great fat
Tears,
Flooding down his face and
Out onto his bed,
Leaving him soaked and
Worn out and
Sullenly
Sodden.

On November the 10th 1999,
Daisy was born and
Daisy died.

But he is crying with
Anger, anger cloaked in the guise of
Sadness.
Anger which gives him a
Rude, aggressive attitude which
Barks and whines and
Tosses him about, making him
Clash with those he wants to soothe.

On November the 10th 1999,
Daisy was born and
Daisy died.

In desperation, he
Kicks and shouts and screams,
He forces his Mum to wake up and
Drag him off to get
Help. He
Laughs and cries. At last,
At last she looks at
Him. She leaves the nightmare of

On November the 10th 1999,
Daisy was born and
Daisy died.

Ollie (5) a nearly adopted boy

Sandy haired, freckled face,
Wide blue eyes,
Engaging smile,
Scabbed knees, scarred elbows.
Solemnly he says, with
Deep welled eyes, 'The
Worst thing is
Shouting and hitting my Dad.'
He is right.
Somewhere,
Clenching and unclenching like a
Cold fist he
Knows that the
Impulse of love draws out of him a
Resonance of
Fear so strong that he is
Impelled to
Destroy that which most he
Desires.

'The next worst thing is
Going Nowhere.'
Again he is right. He puts his
Finger on that sore place and
Picks and picks until it bleeds and
Runs and never heals.
The abuse, the neglect, the fear, that
Chain him, as securely as if
Bound to a chair.
Bind him so
Insecurely that he will
Finally, by going nowhere,
Be sent away.

Josh (10)

I know, I know, I
Rob cars, I
Smash windows, I
Steal from shops, I
Beat up anyone who
Dissatisfies me, I
Shout and swear and scream and
Run off into town,
Jumping from the
High dock wall into the
Deep green greasy water beneath.
Careless of myself.
Not bothered about who I am or
Who you are.

And yet, I know what I want.

What I want is
Respect, says Josh.

Respect is your
Mum and Dad
Tucking you up in bed at night.
You feel
Warm, comforted,
Strengthened and
Safe.

HE IS THE IMAGE OF THE UNSEEN GOD
Form us in the likeness of Your image......

117

Carl (8)

What if the person you are
Angry with is
Dead?

What if in his
Drug-laced life he got himself
Killed?

What if, when the
Gangster pointed the
Gun at his eyes, he did not
Think of his son?

What if in the
Act of dying he was not
Thinking of his son?

What if that means that in his
Lovely stupid life he
Never thought of
Me?

What if I
Never
Knew him?

What if, he, I, his son never......

Oh, so what.

Lucy (8)

My Mum looks at me,
But it's as if I'm not
There. She stares
Through me into the
Middle distance even as she
Calls my name.
(I sometimes catch myself
Turning round to see where I am.)
It's right that she
Sees through me. I'm
Empty, even though I'm
Edged with
Black. That
Black. I scrub and scrub to get
Rid of the
Stain that is me, the
Blot that spoils my mother's
View. But no bleach or brush can
Soften the harsh lines of my
Case.

She says that she loves me, but
If you don't know who someone is,
If you never really see them,
How can you love them?

If I were a
Golden, sun-filled girl, how she would
Love me then. She would
Bask and warm herself at my feet,
Glow in the hazy dust-filled rays,
Sleep contented and
Sure of herself in my
Filtered light. But I am
Empty black,
Scoured black,
Scoured and sour on my mother's
Tongue. Bitter to taste,
Bitter to be.

HE IS THE IMAGE OF THE UNSEEN GOD
Form us in the likeness of Your image . . . . .

119

Ben (7)

I keep my head
Down. Leaning forward
Huddled at the table I
Sleep, absent myself from any
Sharp thought that might
Irritate, provoke,
Remind me just how
Dense the fog is, the
Fog through which I sometimes
Peer with sore eyes. If I
Looked up,
Looked straight at you, the
Whole truth might come
Shockingly,
Splashing out,
Wordlessly, not to be
Contained.

I don't understand,
I don't understand what it all means,
but
I know I'm not good enough, not
Clever enough, and I
Fear I am
UN-UNDERSTANDABLE.

So I live in sequences of
Sly, averted glances,
Evasive turns of head,
Un-focussed looks,
Glazed eyes that further
Clog my clouded mind.

Easier to sleep my life
Away, in case I am
Found out, and
Put to one side,
UN-UNDERSTANDABLE FOR EVER.

HE IS THE IMAGE OF THE UNSEEN GOD
Form us in the likeness of Your image.......

120

Harry (8)

I keep bouncing, bouncing,
Bouncing. From the bed to the
Ceiling, from the ceiling to the
Floor, back up, up,
Up, I
Crash through the attic and
Out to the sky. No-one can
Stop me. I fly, I fly. I

Pee in the corner,
Bang my head,
Punch the walls and
Trash my bread. I
Whine and shout and
Threaten and hide. I

Burn things. I especially like
Burning things.
Paper and wood,
Carpet and coat,
See the match
Flare, smell in the
Smoke. The
Hard, tense flame, the
Fear in my throat.

I keep burning, burning,
Never to stop.
Never to risk
Striking hard earth,
Jolting to stop, a
Helpless sack, a
Sand-filled sack,
Weighted   down   with
All that I want,
All   I   have   lost.

HE IS THE IMAGE OF THE UNSEEN GOD
Form us in the likeness of Your image.......

121

Alex (8)

What are you supposed to
Do with all the
Love you have for somebody, if
That person is
No longer there?
What happens to all that
Left-over-love? Do you
Suppress it,
Ignore it,
Give it to someone else?

I run away.
All the time. I find the
Gap between
Standing at the car door and
Opening it, and I
Run. I
Disappear to
Hold onto a sense of
Who I am. I
Waste my life
Circling and re-circling
Round myself with
Loud, lidless eyes,
Desperate to return home.
I run so I don't have
Chance to think.

Where is home?
Where is it I belong?
Who misses me?
One word repeats itself
Over and over.
Home.

Oh-me, no me.

HE IS THE IMAGE OF THE UNSEEN GOD
Form us in the likeness of Your image......

122

Kelvin (7)

Kelvin's mother says:

'If you go into the
Sea, I would worry about the
Tide. I might
Lose sight of
You. You would not
Hear me over the noise of the
Waves when I
Call. You would not
See me when I
Wave, frantic to
Bring you in.
You might be
Swept out,
Lost for ever.
I would be
Desolate,
Inconsolable.'

Kelvin says:

'It's like that for
Me, when you take
Drugs.'

HE IS THE IMAGE OF THE UNSEEN GOD
Form us in the likeness of Your image. . . . . .

123

Paul (7)

When I was born I was
Much wanted,
Longed for,
Sought after.
But I became a source of
Pain to my Mum.

When I was born I was a
Boy, to be
Favoured, spoilt,
Doted on.
But I was the cause of a
Split in my Dad's family.

When I was born I was
Blue, sick, tired. I
Cracked my Mum's pelvis,
Caused her
Grief. She cried and
Lost her job.

When I was born I was
Not enough, not sufficient.
My Mum says what she wants is
Ivy Eff, a girl,
Intimate and virtuous, not
Me, not Paul.

So now I rage,
Rage with anger and
Remorse.
Red in the face I
Hit my Mum and
Blame myself for not being her
Magical, darling
Ivy Eff.

HE IS THE IMAGE OF THE UNSEEN GOD
Form us in the likeness of Your image......

124

Lisa (14) A childhood legacy.

He snacks on me for
Sex, grazes on my
Body, casually, as he
Passes through the bedroom.
Crunches my bones like
Crisps, hollows out my
Soft parts like a doughnut,
Filling me with a
White, sticky cream. He
Licks my juices and
Forces me to taste him.
Bruises my flesh with
Foxy lips, and
Splits my legs apart like
Chicken wings.
Crushes me into the corner,
Panting in my ear with
Sour, yeasty breath, his
Acrid sweat
Salting my wounds, keeping them
Open and running.

'This is our secret my
Darling one, my
Sweet, my sugar plum.
You and me alone.
If you tell I'll
Kill you like a
Fatted calf,
Roast you whole and
Feed you to the crows. Your
Mum will die, she'll die of
Shame for what you've
Done, for what you've
Tempted me to do.'

So now, my love,
You whom, (terrified), I have
Started to call my love,
When you call me
Darling, dearest,
Sugar plum, you
Know why my body
Freezes, shrinks. Why
Lifeless, I
Lock out.

If I can't say
No, then somehow
You must be my
Dad.

HE IS THE IMAGE OF THE UNSEEN GOD
Form us in the likeness of Your image . . . . .

125

Kevin (6)

She
Relentlessly pursues the
Evidence against me,
Although I am, in
Every sense, just a
Low level traitor. My
Dad, *he* is on the
Higher level, and
He, is still at
Large. No
Injunction stops him. He
Broke her ribs. Now he
Trashes the car,
Bangs on the door at
Midnight,
Roars his hate through the
Letter box.

I have his
Eyes. If only I could
Wash the colour of
His eyes from
Out my eyes. If
Only I could
Cleanse my heart of
His heart. Cut out and
Re-shape the
Curve of my
Lips. Lose the
Male smell that is
Me, the angle in my
Bent neck that is
Him. If

She could only
Kiss that softness
There, that is
Me, not him. When I

Move close,
Sidle up to
Press unseen against her
Knees, she
Screams.

Gill (mother of Kevin)

I'd put up with
Half-way relationships,
Brutal ones,
Ones that came with
Enraged fists and
Spiteful eyes.
That way I
Didn't have to
Worry about
Loneliness.

But then he left, and I
Went into free fall. I
Fell into an
Abyss, a dark chasm where I
Realised I was
All alone.
All alone in the world.

I withdrew to the
Settee. I
Remembered the
Old pain in sudden
Shafts of
New pain.
A pain that
Closes my eyes,
Shuts down my appetite,
Dulls my mind and
Stitches me up in
Shrivelled husks of what I
Used to be.
I become
Un-thinking, un-seeing, un-feeling.

Sometimes I remember I have
Two small boys, and I
Cook them chips and
Maybe beans.

I make do with the
Small change in the
Exchanges of daily living.
I know I
Don't deserve
Anything else.

I used to cry, but
Even that is now
Too much effort.

One day, I will
Just
End it.

HE IS THE IMAGE OF THE UNSEEN GOD
Form us in the likeness of your image . . . . . .

127

Callum (8)

My Mum says I'm
Fit to burn for stealing.
That's how my Mum
Talks about me.
And it's true. I'm
Set on being
Big and dangerous. I
Set fires, I
Break into cars, I
Run off down the town, I
Steal. Mum hides money
Round the house, but it's
Easy. She forgets
How much and
Where. I can find
Twenty pounds. I
Buy friends. I buy them with
Fish and chip dinners. I
Buy sweets. Mum doesn't even
Notice. She doesn't even
Notice big, dangerous
Me.

Can't she hear the
Ripping sound behind my
Eyes? Can't she see that something
Needful and violent
Beats in my brain? A
Sense of longing that
Frightens and consumes me. A
Sense of injury so
Sharpened, and now so exquisitely
Refined, that I register
Outrage on a
Daily basis?

What is
Hardest to bear is that she is
Indifferent to me. She has
Abandoned me. I
Once
Experienced her love, her
Touch, her
Breath upon my

Face. She
Fell under the
Spell of my
Love.

What have I done?
How have I lost her?

Where are you Mum?
Where are you? I

Saw the men who
Beat you up. I
Saw your broken nose and
Eye socket. You
Woke up then, and
Screamed and fought and
Shouted. Maybe, just maybe,
Regretfully, I will have to
Hit you too. I

Really wish I was
Three years old.
Then, I was
Good. But I am
Eight, and
Big and dangerous.

HE IS THE IMAGE OF THE UNSEEN GOD
Form us in the likeness of Your image......

128

Jamie (9)

Sometimes, I think I'm not
Put together right.
Why else would Dad
Sell my toys? Why would he
Take my crisps, keep me
Out in the cold?
Why would he
Hit me? I

Ran away. It was
Night. The streets were
Rough and dark. I
Hid in the
Men's toilets. I got
Cold and hungry, so I
Went back. (I can't say I went
Home.) I
Smashed some windows on the
Way. I
Waited until
Dad came in. He was
Drunk.

Mum's no use. She's a
Witch. I need a mask with
Breathing holes when I'm
Around her.

I think it would be
Nice to be in prison.

HE IS THE IMAGE OF THE UNSEEN GOD
Form us in the likeness of Your image . . . . . .

129

Larry (8)

Dad says he loves me, but
I think he
Doesn't. He
Shouts at me
Too much.
Last time he
Squeezed my hand too
Tight. I think if I
Keep things tidy, my
Mum and Dad might get
Back together.
Mum says she doesn't
Love him, but she
Likes him. So
How can I say I
Don't like him, that I am
Afraid?
(How can you love someone
One minute and
Not love them the next?
Where does all that love
Go?)

At night I can't sleep. I
Worry Dad might
Come back and
Hit me. He
Put my hands once in the
Fire. He says things like
'You'll get put into care.
You'll most likely go to jail.
You'll end up begging
On the streets. I want to
Kill you.'

Sweat breaks out on my
Body.
Worry fires up on my
Brow.
Anxiety crept into my
Heart long ago, and now it
Presses on my

Forehead, and
Lowers itself into my
Eyes.
Lines of thunder
Crease and crackle across my
Face, burning themselves
Deep inside my soul.

Will someone please fix the
Hole in my soul? The
Hole that's getting
Bigger and bigger so I'm
Not sure
Where I begin and where I
End.

Mum says I act
Woeful, - and it's
True. I am
Full of woe.
Deep, angry, active
Woe.

My big worry is…

No, I can't tell you.

(It's Mum might
Leave
Too.)

Gina (11)

Her face was the
First thing I saw,
Tear-stained and dirty,
Eyes blurred into
Blots,
Glistening like
Wet black stones,
Impenetrably difficult to
Read.

It gave me a
Fear of me.

I've never known my
Dad, but I
Think of him
All the time.

Was I so bad, even
Before I was
Born, so he had to
Leave? Is that
Why
Mum
Cries? Because I
Made him
Leave?

Caroline (mother of Jacob).

I am not normally
Aggressive, but when I am
Taunted, I go into
Battle mode.
Words spill out of me like
Caustic soda,
Burning, stinging,
Scorching every thing they
Touch. I know I have
Eyes that are
Looking for a fight.
Battle hard eyes,
Hard and dirty as coal.

I was
Bullied as a
Child, and now I feel
Bitter about my youth,
Bitter about so much
Needless waste,
Waste of me.
I would say that
Now, I have a
Craving for
Bitterness.

If I'm honest, I
Can't wait for
Jacob to stare
Sweet-sour at me,
Defy me,
Show me up in front of my
Friends. Then I can

Snap that hard sweet
Between my teeth and
Feel the
Liquid tide of
Jealousy
Justifiably
Sweep over me and
Out through
Aerated, liberated
Lips and fists.

Arnie and Trisha and Mary and me.

Arnie and Mary were lovers,
Lovely as lovers could be.
Out of their love fell a baby,
A baby boy, Kieran, that's me.

Trisha and Mary were sisters,
Friendly as sisters could be.
Trisha came round for a visit and
Never left, then they were three.

(Apart from me.)

Arnie and Trisha deceived us, they
Snuck off together to play.
Out of their play fell a baby,
A baby boy, Jordan, not me.

Arnie and Trisha and Jordan,
They left us, to live as a three,
Mum and me cried, and we shouted,
But Arnie's not bothered, not he.

So now it's just me and my Mary,
We spend our time sitting at home.
I asked for a pet to look after, I chose
Goldfish who won't ever roam.

Arnie and Trish are my goldfish,
They swim up and down side by side.
Trisha got sick and all spotty,
One day I found she had died.

So Arnie's alone in his fishbowl,
I look at him, looking at me.
He can't ever snick off without me,
I've stuck him just where he should be.

(Looking out for me.)

HE IS THE IMAGE OF THE UNSEEN GOD
Form us in the likeness of Your image.......

133

Colin (6)

I'm standing on the shore,
Dipping my toe in the
Water. Out there
Underneath, I can see
Pink fish,
Strawberry jellies and
Knobbly, purple stars.

Behind me shadows reach out,
Dark rags in a
Grey world. A
Panicky wind is swirling
Sand up from the edge, blowing
Grit in my eyes.

Inside me my
Heart squeezes painfully, a
Heart full of broken glass.
Will I always have to walk
Straight through each day and
Out through each night, in a
Desolation - born of
Seeing a bright coloured world
Tantalisingly there on the
Edge of the grey I
Permanently inhabit?

My red heart turns
Black. I try to
Free myself in one
Swift jump, a
Frustrated punch at my
Mum's head.

But now, sadly, I know
Something of the
Internal dust storm I
Carry within, and how I
Persist in greying my own
World.

Nora, mother of Colin

She gazed at me in
Bullish expectation. Her
Face was strident with the need to
Attack. But, for me, the
Sadness of drink and solitude was
Loud in her,
Pressing out through
Bright, hurt eyes,
Massed in her
Tangled hair and
Loose, cheap tracksuit.

'I can think back if I'm asked to,'
She said, 'but
Back is confused,
Back is a story that causes
Pain. Best to
Smother it,
Blot it out in a
Slurry of drink.
That way, sometimes, I can
Fool myself I've got a life,
Some sort of life, even when the
Curdled, polluted fluid
Boils in my throat, and with a
Shudder, I
Taste myself.

Sadness and anger
Fizz and buzz like
Acid in my veins. I'm
Scared. If I start, I
Know I'll be like a
Child, picking at a scab.
Picking, picking. I

Won't be able to leave it
Alone. I'll have to
Flip the top off,
See the blood rise. I'll have to
Extract the most pain,
Pain that will rip and tear at the
Padding I've so carefully
Wound round my heart.

(Some things come with their
Own punishments.)

The trouble is I only have to
See him, and I lose my cool,
Lose my centre as that
Other man
Stares out of his
Eyes.

Lee (8)

Do I dare,
Have I the right, to
Breathe,
Take up space,
Be me?

(I lived with my Mum on the
Steps of the town. She
Died when I was two.)

Distress in me takes on a
Damaged quality, a dimension of
Longing, that sadly,
Reveals the original wound.

(On the steps of the town I
Lived with my Mum.)

I used to feel my body
Change, just from being
Next to her, within the
Smell and feel of her. But she was
Careless with me, she
Forgot me for a moment, and
Died.

(I want to die and
Live with my Mum.)

Now I am skilled at
Blanking myself off. I go
Quite still and
Hide my face.
Nobody can see,
Nobody picks me out, I am
Safe.

(On the steps of the town she
Forgot me, took her drug, and
Died.) She didn't even

Turn and wave
Goodbye. She
Left me behind, without
Foundation,
Condemned to live forever, in my
Mind, on the
Cold, hard surface of the
Steps of the
Town.

My anger has been in
Cold storage. It has been
Bubbling under a
Crust of ice,
Suppressing some
Good memory too, that
Needs to be hidden, lest the
Fresh air soil it. But

Will I always be this
Little, naked, scared person
Crashing through the woods?
Will the twin monsters of
Loneliness and fear always
Haunt my dreams?

(On the steps of the town she
Forgot me and
Died.)

If I risk acknowledging my
Deep need, will I
Disappear too? I'm
Frightened that the
Little air I have will be
Sucked away, that the
Wings I've sprouted so suddenly
will
Tear me into shreds.

(She forgot me and
Died.)

HE IS THE IMAGE OF THE UNSEEN GOD
Form us in the likeness of Your image......

136

Milly (10)

I don't know where the hit
Comes from. I didn't know I
Had the hit in me. But it is
Out now. Perhaps it is
Anger,
Anger which will have to be
Held.
Held, resentfully, for ever,
Because there is
No place to
Lay it down,
No one to give it to.

In my Mum there is an
Absence, an
Abyss where
Anger should be. She is
Economical, practical. With
Complete and composed
Efficiency she
Organises the hit. It's not
Personal, not personal to
Me, oh no. She is
Driven by fear,
Fear of how
Powerless she is, and how
Powerful I am. So she seeks
Subtly, to
Destroy in me what she can not
Subdue.

In a way, she tries to
Attract the attention she thinks she
Deserves, through me. Whereas I, I
Hit to make sure I
Deserve the attention I already
(Unfairly), receive.

Afterwards she makes up with a
Hug, a hug that feels like a
Push, a
Kiss that feels like a
Smack. A
Cloudy kiss, a kiss that demands a
Kiss-back.

HE IS THE IMAGE OF THE UNSEEN GOD
Form us in the likeness of Your image . . . . .

137

Terry (8)

The end doesn't
Turn out like I
Expected.
Balls thrown high in the
Air, come down
Behind me.
Presents at Christmas
Under the tree, just
Might go to
Someone else at the
Last minute. Then I get
Angry, and I'm so
Busy being angry I can't
Stop long enough to
Try out being good and
See if that feels
Better.

Mum wants me to
Keep the rules, but
My life isn't that
Orderly. It
Runs about all over the place,
In and out and
Roundabout.
Words fly out of my
Mouth. They
Bite my Mum and then
Come back and bite
Me.
Everything I touch goes
Galloping off in every direction,
Leaving me
Staring, shocked and
Open-mouth-mazed. I am
Tormented, talkative,
Consumed by ideas.

When I make a
Mistake, how can I
Stop it happening
Again? I'm
Sad, because I can't
Find a way to be

Good. It's hard to
Think, even how to
Start. My
Thinking head so
Easily floats away. Then I
Can't remember, even that I
Want to be good.

I'm Mr.
Forget-terry.

Terry and anxiety

A sparkler my Mum
Hands me,
Flares and showers
Fire over my
Frightened fingers.

(I have a sister who never
Sees my Dad.)

Mum might
Gobble me up like a
Delicious ice-cream. I'll
Melt on her tongue and
Disappear forever.

(Will my Dad pretend he
Doesn't know
Me too one day?)

"Whatever possesses you?" she
Screams, 'Whatever
Possesses you?'

'You do', I think in
Terror, 'You do.'
Better to kick and jump and
Fizz, than to
Stay still and be
Trapped or
Disappeared for
Ever.

HE IS THE IMAGE OF THE UNSEEN GOD
Form us in the likeness of Your image......

138

Aiden (10)

I am so busy,
Busy being not bothered.
Cast adrift in my own
Confused world. I have
Arrived at a place where
Time has stopped at
Winter, my mind bare and
Empty as the leafless trees
Bending in the wind.
I have lost the
Thread of things. I seem to
Sleep all day, and yet I am
Tired, dark-eyed with a
Hunger that consumes me with a
Lifetime of emotion, still
Unused.

I can see in her eyes that she
Wishes me
Dead. But she is my
Mother and should
Love me, but does
Not, nor ever will.

I stare inwards, I
Stare out. In both places I find
Desolation.

Tori, mother of Aiden

'Let me ask you an old
Riddle.' she says.
'My father has a
Son. Who is he to me?'
'Simple,' I say. 'He is your
Brother.'
'That may be so' she says, 'But
I know he is also my
Son.' She looks at me
Carefully. She sees the
Blush and shock
Rise in my eyes and face. She sees
Pity and concern and she
Rejects them.

'I do not want your
Bounty. Let me tell you
How it is.

My son grabs
Greedily and voraciously at my
Breasts, as
He did. I am
Confused. All that was once so
Hateful to me, (yet
Dazzled me too,) now
Coalesces in him. He
Craves my milk, - the
Milk of human kindness, but
I do not love him, - yet.
There, I've said it. The
One truth that now
Struggles with all the
Lies, lies told over the
Years that
Compete with each other to
Confuse and ensnare. I

Howl my loss into the
Cold, bitter air that
Hangs between us.'

HE IS THE IMAGE OF THE UNSEEN GOD
Form us in the likeness of Your image ....

139

Conrad (8)

I worry about nature and the
World and the
Bad things happening to
Birds and dolphins.
People treat the world like
Dirt.

I was four.
I didn't see the fight but I
Heard the bang, and then I saw
Mum sitting on the bed
Crying, and Dad's drunken head
Gashed and open, the
Blood meeting the broken
Glass on the floor and the
Hole in the wall and Dad's
Crushed knuckles, and Mum
Crying and crying. I

Wished with all my heart that I could
Crawl into her,
Place myself between her and her own
Damage, absorb the
Bruises for her, - and the
Big bruise of
Being herself. She

Told him to go, and I'm
Glad, (because he used to
Smack my head too, and
Punch my stomach and
Squeeze me too tight,) but I still

Worry all the time. Something
Bad might happen. Something
Bad might happen if I'm
Not there.

HE IS THE IMAGE OF THE UNSEEN GOD
Form us in the likeness of Your image.......

140

Richard (10)

In my dreams my
Mind is running full tilt
Towards the cliff,
Blood pounding in my ears,
Hot air rasping my throat, my
Legs leaden and dragging.

I overhang myself and gaze
Horrified into the
Black depths where
Snakeish arms of bullies
Writhe and threaten. The
School gate
Clangs behind me.
I am on the edge of
Falling from this
Dizzy precipice.

To fall is too easy.

I look
Back along the cliff path, and see my
Safety rope untied, my
Family in the distance beginning the
Long goodbye. I

Jump.

HE IS THE IMAGE OF THE UNSEEN GOD
Form us in the likeness of Your image . . . . . .

141

Max (5)

The thing is, it's like
This.
I wake up in the morning,
In the game, and I'm on
Square 15 and I have to
Choose.

Do I want to
Sleep with a dead body for
One minute, or do I
Go through a forest, with a
Dead body hanging from a
Tree, and risk being
Hoovered up by
Alien aircraft?

You choose, Hermione,
You choose.

It's like this with Mum and Darren or
Dad and Lesley.
How do I choose?

Sometimes it's best to be
King Bomb and
Explode and
Destroy the game,

Until the
Next time.

.

Cleo (8)

A tale of Dads and other confusions

I carry
Family secrets in every
Limb of my body.
Consider how things began. (A
Particular beginning results in a
Particular end.)
My beginning is
Rooted in violence,
Hitting, shouting, shame.

My **sister's** Dad
Played with her. He played to
Hurt, to confuse and defile. He
Played to pleasure himself,
Poking his fingers in her soft
Hidden parts. He left her with
Nightmares. He got sent to
Jail.

My **brother's** Dad is my Mum's
Uncle. My brother has
Learning difficulties.

My Dad hit my
Mum, hit my
Brother. Now my brother
Hits me, (but they say it's not
His fault.)

Now we have a new Dad, - but
Can anything good come out of
Dads, I wonder?

What chance is there for
Me?
Sometimes I feel as if
Blood is pouring out of my
Ears.

HE IS THE IMAGE OF THE UNSEEN GOD
Form us in the likeness of Your image.......

143

Tom (8)

Will you just
Chill out Mum?
Can't you see I'm
Busy, busy watching
Cricket?
You could learn from me.
Learn to sit, to
Gaze, to be silent.
What are you afraid of? I
Wish you would
Shake out that
Famished, fragment of a person I
See you think you are.
Lay yourself out to dry.
Lift your face.
Look at the sun!
Sing to me.
Sing in your husky
Cigarette-laden voice
Songs of love and
Honey.

HE IS THE IMAGE OF THE UNSEEN GOD
Form us in the likeness of Your image......

144

Sylvie (8)

All around me
Spins. I see
Peripherally and at
Great speed.
Words
Tumble out of me.
Stories and fancies
Crowd my head.

(My Dad in lipstick,
Green eye shadow,
Droplet earrings
Swinging about my head as he
Hovers over and
Around my bed.)

I fill my pants on a
Daily basis with fearful,
Stinking shit. I
Know I smell and am
Not worth
Protecting.

Stories fill the
Emptiness left by
Loss of my Mum.
Day and night I
Clutch them to myself to
Ward off the fearful
Dark places the other side of
Silence.

HE IS THE IMAGE OF THE UNSEEN GOD
Form us in the likeness of Your image . . . . .

145

Gina (5)

Basal ganglia,
Epilepsy, - such
Cruel, clanging,
Clashing words, but they
Do not, cannot
Tell of my sense of the
Peril in which my
Mum lives, equalled only by
My fear of increasing it.
Me, - an unforeseen
Danger in her way. I
Can't conquer that
Terror of myself when I see how
Frightened she is of
Me.

We play a fearful
Game of ring a roses. Our
Linked hands
Push us hard apart. Our
Singing fills the air with
Lament. I feel myself
Falling, falling,
Never to return.

The love I feel
Rises in my throat,
Blocks the air. I long to
Cover her mouth with
My mouth,
Drink her in. But
Fear and rage,
Like monsters, rise up and
Tear us,
Rip us apart.

Douglas (9)

This strange world! This place of
Subtle affinities,
Coloured meanings, so
Strange to one who deals in
Black and white.

Where is the implicit understanding
Between the
Hand that opens and the
Arm it touches? Between
Daniel and his Mum?

I have always felt I live
Under a
Bomb that threatens to
Drop on me. I know, because
Daily shards
Splinter the air
Glancing dangerously
Off my face.

My Mum is full of
Rules,
Interior rules that
Spring out and
Explode in my face. Her
Temper upends me. I'm
Flung about, unable to keep my
Balance. In my head
Stones spill from the skies.

I know that I have brought
No joy at any time to
Any one, that I
Fill a place in the house that
She would like to be
Empty.

Sometimes I see her as a
Mound of sparkling,
Jewelled jelly. She
Spoons the liquid drops
Onto my tongue.

Only then do I taste the
Bitterness of poison
Spreading through my soul.

Jed (6)

Death steps out of the
Shadows, looks me in the
Eye and challenges me for a
Place on my Mum's lap.

My inside-out love
Crosses and weaves its
Complex patterns of
Care,
Snagging on the
Razor blades she
Slides into her arms.

Hungry, I press into her
Side,
Wrap my arms around her
Neck,
Bite and bruise her in my
Desperate bid for
Love.

But Death steps closer,
Takes my Mum by the hand and
Leads her
Away.

Alone and unloved,
Who else can I strike in
Retribution but
Myself?

Carter and the ice-cream man (6)

That man there,
He is the ice-cream man. He
Plays the tune and I
Come running, even though I
Know the white, sticky
Flowering on his
Cone will not be
Sweet to taste but
Bitter. Not a
Cool, refreshing slide down my
Throat, but a
Hot, pulsing that
Clogs my mouth and
Fogs my mind.

But then, I was born
Addicted, they tell me.
(Addicted to what? I wonder.
Addicted to ice cream?)
All I know is the
Fear I feel when I
Breathe his borrowed breath,
Soak up his spreading stain, the
Confusing stain of
Desolation and relief. A

Reddening shame rises and
Fights the
Part of me that
Longs to be the
Ice-cream boy, who
Plays the tune and has them
Running to lick my
Cone. No tears can
Rinse away the
Grief of my frozen isolation now.

Jim (10)

I am
Dangerous to know,
Dangerous to love, the
Whole look of me is
Perilous.

There exists a
Violent flame-hot
Blade-sharp kind of
Fear that
Crashes through my eyes and
Explodes in my face.
Anxiety catches as a
Bundle of barbed wire
Deep within my ribcage. A
Lostness in my eyes
Reveals a
Dead space where memories should
Lie. The small
Flickering of a
Storm crossing my face
Masks the collapse that
Pulls and tears
Threatening to erupt in a
Flurry of hardened fists.

I
Brew my anger down,
Boiling it into a
Thick potent tar to
Trap my victims in and find
Myself
Helplessly, hopelessly
Stuck in the mire.

HE IS THE IMAGE OF THE UNSEEN GOD
Form us in the likeness of Your image......

150

Sariya (2)

In May, the
First cold rains of autumn
Rattled against my
Window. My Dad went
Out and never came back. So,
With stiff fingers I
Press his body into the
Cold sand, cover his head with a
Stone. Then
Grief absconded with my
Mum. She cannot
See me through the
Curtain of tears that
Falls about her face. My

Dance from the
Cradle had only just begun.
I was learning how the
World was connected, how
I was connected, when
Suddenly all logic and
Reason flew away. So

Who will now
Shelter me from the
Rain storm? Who
Save me from the
Heat at noon day? Who will
Cut through the bars of
Iron that
Deploy across my soul?

At whose feet may I safely
Lay my love? In
Whose lap
Bury my head?

HE IS THE IMAGE OF THE UNSEEN GOD
Form us in the likeness of Your image . . . . .

151

Vanessa (12)

You are there, a
Shadow against my own,
Following me at every turn,
Bent on carrying absence. I become
Undone by a smell, a word, a
Place, by a love that
Calls my name while
Looking the other way. I could
Sit next to you on a bus,
Brush past you in a shop,
Stand silently behind you in a queue. I

Cross through the boundary of
Skin, a soft apple bruise
Spreading, thickening, darkening.

'Don't cry, don't cry.' This
Easy emission of blood, let
This be in place of tears. I
Have not been selected for
Life, I have been
Selected for death.
It is what I don't have that
Dominates my life,
What is missing that
Shapes everything I do. A
Dark blue sleep
Shuts my eyes. I gaze
Ahead, directly into
Oblivion.

Karl (10)

'This is my lucky day,' I say, although
I cannot bear it. The poignant
Tide of pain that
Sweeps to meet me. The
Blank hunted look in the
Child's staring eyes
Gazing from his delicate
Skeletal head.
They seem to code an
SOS, to code and
Scramble, before I have
Chance to
Construe.
The eyes of someone who's been a
Long time
Hopelessly
Drowned.

Gravely he says from
Within his pain,
'This is my lucky day too'.

The pit of my stomach
Tightens, falls. I
Take his hands.
Coming to him
Empty. I go away
Filled.
Give me your pain and I will
Hold it. I will
Not
Pass it on. This is my
Gethsemane, our
Calvary.

Marc (7)

(For God alone my soul in silence
waits.)

Marc,
Huddled in his chair,
Sulkily pouting,
Arms folded in strict defiance
Holding himself in and holding
Me out.

I wait: in the completeness of
Silence.
He is mourning,
Mourning his loss.
Looking into the void.
There is no consolation.
No-one who can
Comfort him.
I can only
Enter his solitude and
Wait.

I do not touch his face or his
Hand. (There didn't seem to be
Any place to touch.)
I cannot get too near him.
He might have to
Face me, look at me,
Dreadfully smile and
Answer to me. I will not
Ask him to
Speak of his
Unspeakable grief.
He is facing the Eternal,
Solidly alone,
Comfortless. There is
No noise,
No activity that can
Cover this.

The Garden

There are more things in life than we can
Touch or see.

If you find a garden in someone's
Mind, believe it.
Accept it as a gift.
Take care of it.
Help it develop and flourish.
Celebrate having found this garden.
And know that when it is time to leave,
The gardener,
Whom you cannot see,
Will be there, as He was before,
Faithfully tending and nurturing it,
And other helpers will come as you
Did,
And play their part in caring for the
Garden.

HE IS THE IMAGE OF THE UNSEEN GOD
Form us in the likeness of Your image......

155

HE IS THE IMAGE OF THE UNSEEN GOD
Form us in the likeness of Your image......

156

BIOGRAPHICAL NOTES.

Desmond, eight years old, had been abused and rejected by his Mum and had lived all his life with his grandparents. His grandfather had recently died. Desmond had found his body on the settee. He was terrified that his grandmother would die too and that he would have no-one left in the whole world to love him.

Maria, aged ten, lived with both her parents, but finally disclosed an enduring history of physical and sexual abuse by her Dad. Her Mum had chosen to ignore the evidence before her eyes. Maria was one of three siblings, but she was picked out as the victim of her Dad's violence.

Timmy, aged 6, had a Mum who was a drug addict and a prostitute. Timmy lived in a fantasy world where he imagined that he could rescue his Mum and live happily ever after. He was often left for periods of time in a Children's Home when his Mum couldn't cope with him. **Leaving** describes his feelings when he has to leave his therapist, heightened feelings and understanding of himself as worthless and deserving of rejection. This ending mirrors the fear of final extermination of self that he is driven by.

Keith, aged eight, terrorised the school and neighbourhood with his destructiveness and cruelty. He lived with the memories of his Dad beating up his Mum and the consequent terror of this man, his Dad, that they all lived with. In his world, to admit to feelings of fear or helplessness was a sign of weakness. He acted out his fear in extremely aggressive ways instead.

Ali, aged ten, and in care while his Mum was in prison for neglect of her children. (One of Ali's siblings had died.) He describes being continuously raped and abused, but for him, the memories of his Mum, and the neglect that put him in care, her incapacity and unavailability to be a source of comfort and strength to him, was the worst thing to bear.

Simon, aged seven, had a head whirling with questions about himself and his Dad. He had witnessed many severe instances of domestic violence. He was tortured by thoughts of the possibility that he might be like his Dad. He feared his Dad, yet mourned his loss. He was hyperactive and inattentive.

Kristy, aged eight, sexually abused by her step-dad, emotionally neglected and abandoned by her Mum, brought up by step grandparents who did not believe her, despite their son being convicted and given a prison sentence, full of guilt when her Dad committed suicide in prison, expresses the paramount pain of rejection.

Lena, aged seven, begins to articulate her uncertainty about being loved, and the ensuing uncertainty over whether she herself truly loves her Mum.

HE IS THE IMAGE OF THE UNSEEN GOD
Form us in the likeness of Your image......

157

David, aged eight, shows the fury of betrayal, rage at his Mum's lack of protection of him, and his own little boy helplessness at not being able to protect his Mum.

James, aged four, reveals his horrific history of physical abuse. He repeats the pattern in self-destruction, while showing graphically how near he is to complete disintegration.

Basil, aged seven, witness to domestic violence, a mother on drugs, Dad a Schedule 1 Offender, fights to stay alive.

Darren, aged nine, shows the bewilderment of physical abuse and the chilling knowledge that he could repeat the pattern when he becomes an adult and possible a parent.

Grace, aged two, is refusing to communicate or show interest in speaking. She experiences a Mum who is detached and unavailable to be that Mum for whom she longs. She can see and touch her Mum, but cannot get near her.

John, aged nine, thought that he was the reason his Mum and Dad had split up. It was because they could not cope with him and his hyperactive behaviour. He was the cause of all their quarrels. He was resentful of his diagnosis (ADHD) and resisted taking his medication.

Mikey, aged ten, acted the clown, the joker, always teasing, tricking and upsetting people. His exterior clowning hid a very sad boy, unsure of his position in the household, deeply jealous of his Mum's new partner and their baby. He felt he had lost many things.

Carole, aged 6, had a Mum who was terrified for her children, imagining all sorts of dangers awaiting them. To ensure that she was a good Mum and to keep the professional network active around her, she ascribed various illnesses to them. Carole was designated oppositional and aggressive, destructive and disobedient and in need of CAMHS support. She was in fact a bright and parental child, fully aware of the enmeshed relationship she had with her Mum, which she both wanted and rejected.

Danny, aged ten, suffered from enuresis and encupresis. He found this humiliating and distressing. It stemmed from his witnessing his violent Dad hitting his Mum and the feelings of impotence and rage that this left him with.

Louis, aged seven, was badly teased and bullied at school. His Mum was an alcoholic and drug addict and had lost custody of him. He lived with his Gran who was old and couldn't cope with him. He was failing at school and haunted by the fear that he was a copy of his violent Dad.

Miles, aged eight, had a sister, Daisy who died at birth at home. Miles had been there. His Mum sunk into an inconsolable grief and neglected herself and the other children in the family. Miles became wild and uncontrollable to try and force her into paying attention to him.

Ollie, aged five, had had nine care placements up the age of three. Now he was with a family who wanted to adopt him. They had recently had a new baby of their own. This stimulated fears and longings in Ollie which spilled over in aggressive behaviour, so much so that his adoption was being put in jeopardy.

Josh, aged ten, lived with his Mum and Dad. His Dad worked long hours as an electrician. His Mum suffered from depression. Josh felt he was unimportant to both of them in their separate ways. His Dad was never there. His Mum was sunk in her own depression. Josh ran wild round the neighbourhood, truanting from school and hanging out in gangs. He clearly identified what he was missing in his life, love and attention from his parents.

Carl, aged eight, had a Dad who had been killed in a drug related gang fight. There was a conspiracy of silence in the family about his Dad and his death. Carl was tormented by thoughts of his Dad and whether his Dad had ever truly loved him or thought about him.

Lucy, aged eight, had a Mum who had been shocked to find herself pregnant and then increasingly resentful of a baby who had 'taken away her life, taken away her job, taken away who she wanted to be'. Lucy felt guilty at having done this. She suffered from obsessional compulsive disorder in which she scrubbed herself incessantly, cleaned the house obsessively and searched the shops for different cleaning materials. She was lonely and found it difficult to make friends.

Ben, aged seven, had specific learning difficulties. He knew that somehow he did not fit into the expected world of school. He feared the impatience of his parents with him, and preferred to hide under a cloak of mild depression rather than face his anxieties. He experienced himself as un-understandable.

Harry, aged eight, with a diagnosis of ADHD, hyperactive with a limited attention span, further complicated by having a Mum and step Dad who were worn out trying to cope with him. Confusingly while being told that it was not his fault, (he had 'something wrong with his brain'), Harry was often punished for his behaviour. He felt unwanted and reacted in an ever increasing whirl of oppositional anxiety.

Alex, aged eight, had a Dad who had walked away from the family. Alex felt this acutely as a reflection on himself. He coped with these feelings by truanting and running away from home. He engaged in ever more risky and dangerous behaviours. His Mum felt she had no control over him.

HE IS THE IMAGE OF THE UNSEEN GOD
Form us in the likeness of your image......

159

Kelvin, aged seven, lived with a Mum addicted to heroin. He draws an exact parallel between her anxieties if he were to swim in the sea and the fears induced in him by her taking drugs. He might lose her for ever one day.

Paul, aged seven, had been told many stories about his birth. In spite of being much wanted, his birth had cause dissension in the families. His birth had been difficult and had left his Mum with on-going health problems. He was constantly told that his Mum wanted a girl using IVF.

Lisa, aged fourteen, on the brink of her first intimate adolescent relationship, describes the source of her fears which lie in childhood sexual abuse by her Dad.

Kevin, aged six, had a Mum who had been severely abused by his Dad. Kevin was a constant reminder to her of this violent man. She found it impossible to see Kevin as a separate little boy, desperate for her love and affection.

Gill, Kevin's mother, describes the loss of her previous violent relationship, with her ensuing loneliness, depression and suicidal thoughts.

Callum, aged eight, begins to think that being aggressive and oppositional is not sufficient to awaken his Mum out of the torpor into which she has sunk. He sees that she still goes out with violent men and begin to consider imitating their behaviour, by hitting his Mum. Perhaps then she would choose to spend time with him.

Jamie, aged nine, blames himself for the cruelty and neglect he experiences from his parents. He thinks longingly of an imagined safety and containment in prison.

Larry, aged eight, still goes to stay at weekends with a sadistic Dad who hurts him physically and mentally. The thought that his Mum might abandon him and he would have to live permanently with his Dad, terrorises him.

Gina, aged eleven, had a Mum who had had post natal depression. Gina felt she had never been able to reach her Mum. She thinks it must be because of her inherent wickedness that her Dad left her before she was even born, and her Mum remains unreachable.

Caroline, mother of Jacob, aged ten, begins to understand why she is so harsh towards her own son, harsh and yet over protective. Jacob resents both these ways of treating him. He begins to emulate the bullies who spoilt his Mum's school days.

Kieran, aged seven, lived alone with his Mum. His Dad had gone off with his Mum's sister. They had set up house round the corner and had a new family. Kieran was furious at his Dad's deceptive and disloyal behaviour while also desperate to keep close to him. He plays these feelings out as he gazes at his pet goldfish.

Colin, aged six, lived with a Mum who was an alcoholic. His violent Dad had left, but Colin was still expected to see him. He escapes into an imaginary world, filled with colour and light. He tries to break free from his grey world by being violent himself while also realising that his actions only serve to increase the greyness inside him.

Nora, mother of Colin, talks about her painful memories, her drunkenness, and the constant reminder of those previous violent days when she looks into Colin's eyes.

Lee, aged eight, had a Mum who half lived on the streets and who died of septicaemia from drug use when Lee was two. Anxious and fearful, Lee withdraws from life, not willing to risk himself in relationship again, and yet mourning his loss.

Milly, aged ten, was in an enmeshed reciprocally violent relationship with her Mum. To get her own needs met, her Mum dragged Milly round medical services, creating stories of hurt and anger to justify their attendance. Milly correctly identified her Mum's need to get help via her daughter.

Terry, aged eight, comes across as chaotic and wayward, forgetful and anxious. In the second snapshot he reveals that he has discovered that his Dad has a daughter whom he disowns, (has forgotten about?) Could this happen to him he wonders.

Aiden, aged ten, the product of an incestuous relationship, knows he is not loved but cannot make sense of it. In her poem, Aiden's Mum, **Tori,** reveals the source of both their anguish.

Conrad, aged eight, remembers the domestic violence he witnessed so often. He fears for his Mum and grieves over what she has suffered. As a result he is hyper vigilant and over-protective of her. He actively and physically fights for her.

Richard, aged ten, is terrified of moving to secondary school. He fears being bullied. He fears not being able to do the work. He is ready to do something desperate and self harming to escape the situation. His parents do not listen to him or take his fears seriously.

Max, aged five, describes his life as in a board game. He has momentous and impossible decisions to make. Who should he live with? How can he possibly choose? He sees himself helpless, caught in a lifetime of impossible decisions. He shows his unhappiness in explosive and disruptive behaviour.

Cleo, aged eight, describes the many men she has as Dad. Her Dad was violent; her sister's Dad sexually abused her; her brother's Dad is her Mum's brother. Now her Mum has a new partner, a new Dad for Cleo. What is she to think of him? How is she to behave? What chance has she got?

Tom, aged eight, wishes his Mum would cast off her busy, intrusive behaviour and return to the Mum he remembers from when he was a little, a Mum who sang to him, and enjoyed being with him.

Sylvie, aged eight, lives in a household riddled with secrets. He Dad is a transvestite and possibly abuses her. Her Mum copes by being detached and distant. Sylvie soils herself and is dirty and unkempt. Her peers reject her. She fills her life and head with a protective whirl of fancies and stories.

Gina, aged five, born with many disabilities, understands the fear she generates in her Mum. She senses her Mum trying hard to be a good Mum to her, but nothing can conceal the fundamental feeling of loss of love and disappointment. Fear and rage fill the air between them.

Douglas, aged nine, has Asperger's syndrome. He doesn't understand the world he inhabits. His Mum has similar characteristics and tries to impose order on an unintelligible world with hundreds of rules. Douglas bears the brunt of her tempers when things spin out of control.

Jed, aged five, has a Mum who self harms. He blames himself for not being that precious boy for whom she would choose to live. He begins to imitate her self harming behaviour.

Carter, aged six, was born addicted to heroin as a result of his Mum taking drugs when she was pregnant. He has been sexually abused and sees himself caught in a pattern of replicative behaviour, which is, confusingly, both reassuring and shameful.

Jim, aged ten, is fiercely angry in discovering, at the age of ten, that the man he thought was his Dad is not in fact his Dad. He finds his real Dad and is rejected by him. He has lost his sense of self, his sense of who he is. The memories he has are false memories. He burns with an anger that in the end is merely self destructive.

Sariya, aged two, struggles to understand where her Dad has gone. He died of cancer, and her Mum is incapacitated by grief. So Sariya experiences a double loss.

Vanessa, aged twelve, lives with her Dad who is alcoholic and violent. Her Mum died when she was nine. Vanessa's last memory is of quarrelling with her Mum. In her guilt she cuts herself, and has tried to hang herself.

HE IS THE IMAGE OF THE UNSEEN GOD
Form us in the likeness of Your image......

162

Karl, aged ten, was the youngest of a huge family of boys, who ran riot in the neighbourhood. He was ragged, undernourished, and streetwise and also acutely aware of his lowly status in society. In our meeting he senses a new beginning.

Marc, aged seven, had lived in the care system from the age of two, having been neglected and abused by his natural parents. He has built up a protective shell to defend himself against the possibility of getting close to someone and being betrayed.

POSTSCRIPT

The book as a whole is a journey towards the 'visible presence of God',

in Old Testament terms the 'glory' of God,

as we encounter Him in our lives and the lives of others.

Give us a spirit of wisdom and revelation as we come to know You,

so that, with the eyes of our hearts enlightened,

we may know what is the hope to which You have called us.

The Letter to the Ephesians 1. 17-18.

HE IS THE IMAGE OF THE UNSEEN GOD
Form us in the likeness of Your image . . . . .

163